DRAMA CLASSICS

The Drama Classics series aims to offer the world's greatest plays in affordable paperback editions for students, actors and theatregoers. The hallmarks of the series are accessible introductions, uncluttered texts and an overall theatrical perspective.

Given that readers may be encountering a particular play for the first time, the introduction seeks to fill in the theatrical/historical background and to outline the chief themes rather than concentrate on interpretational and textual analysis. Similarly the play-texts themselves are free of footnotes and other interpolations: instead there is an end-glossary of 'difficult' words and phrases.

The texts of the English-language plays in the series have been prepared taking full account of all existing scholarship. The foreign-language plays have been newly translated into a modern English that is both actable and accurate: many of the translators regularly have their work staged professionally.

Edited until his early death by Kenneth McLeish, the Drama Classics series continues with his aim of providing a first-class library of dramatic literature representing the best of world theatre.

Associate editors:
Professor Trevor R. Griffiths
Dr. Colin Counsell
School of Arts and Humanities
University of North London

DRAMA CLASSICS *the first hundred*

*The publishers welcome
suggestions for further titles*

DRAMA CLASSICS

CHILDREN OF THE SUN

by

Maxim Gorky

translated and with an introduction by
Stephen Mulrine

London
NICK HERN BOOKS
www.nickhernbooks.co.uk

A Drama Classic

This edition of *Children of the Sun* first published in Great Britain as a paperback original in 1999 by Nick Hern Books Limited, 14 Larden Road, London W3 7ST

Copyright in the introduction © 2000 Nick Hern Books

Copyright in this translation © 2000 Stephen Mulrine

Typeset by Country Setting, Kingsdown, Kent CT14 8ES
Printed by Bath Press, Avon

A CIP catalogue record for this book is available from the British Library

ISBN 1 85459 429 X

Introduction

Maxim Gorky (1868-1936)

It is difficult to imagine a more colourful life than that of Maxim Gorky, and that is not simply due to his involvement in some of this century's most dramatic events, or his complex relationships with Lenin and Stalin. Born Alexei Maximovich Peshkov, on 16 March 1868, in the bustling Volga port of Nizhny Novgorod, Gorky led an extraordinary life almost from infancy. His early years are described in the three volumes of autobiography which are justly regarded as among his greatest achievements.

Gorky's maternal grandparents owned a small dye-works in Nizhny, and after the death of his father, his mother abandoned the four year-old Gorky to his grandparents' care. The treatment he endured there at the hands of his brutish grandfather was little short of child abuse, and soon after his mother's death in 1879, Gorky, at the age of eleven, was sent out of the family home to earn his living.

The bare record of Gorky's employment, over the next decade, makes fascinating reading – errand boy, birdcatcher, domestic servant, dishwasher on a Volga steamship, apprentice icon-painter, night-watchman, stevedore, bakery hand. During this time, Gorky sought constantly to expand his mental horizons, not only through books, but also people, engaging in the fierce political debate soon to bear fruit in revolution.

In that respect, Gorky's experiences in Kazan were particularly formative. Gorky had gone there in the autumn of 1884, in the hope of entering the university, and though he failed to gain admission, he succeeded in mixing with a wide range of people, including political radicals, of the sort who would later provide the left, 'Bolshevik' wing of the Social Democrats. Gorky was unhappy in Kazan, however, and although his reasons are unclear – a disappointment in love, perhaps, or news of his grandmother's death - he tried to commit suicide by shooting himself in the heart, on 12 December 1887, at the age of nineteen. Fortunately, he missed his aim, but the bullet pierced his lung, leaving him permanently prone to ill-health.

The following spring, working in a provincial village bakery, Gorky took a more active role in politics, joining a moderate reform group, the People's Right, committed to raising peasant consciousness. The experience served only to reinforce what was to be a lifelong distrust of the peasantry, and Gorky soon gave up the struggles, to embark on a lengthy trek through South Russia. At Tsaritsyn in 1889, where he found employment as a railway nightwatchman, Gorky came under the spell of Tolstoy, and went so far as to write to the great man, begging him for land on which to create a 'Tolstoyan' utopian commune. He received no reply, and a visit to Tolstoy's estate proved equally fruitless.

Gorky then returned to his home town of Nizhny, which was rapidly becoming a focus of radical politics, with exiled students from Moscow and Kazan, and was immediately placed under police surveillance. He was even imprisoned for a time, and only his damaged lung prevented his being conscripted into the army. In April 1891, Gorky left Nizhny to begin another cross-country odyssey, stocking his capacious mind with the people and places which would soon nourish his writing.

At Tiflis in Georgia, Gorky's first short story, *Makar Chudra*, appeared in a local newspaper on 12 September 1892. Widely acclaimed, it not only launched his literary career, it also introduced him to the world under his nom-de-plume, 'Maxim Gorky', i.e., 'Maxim the Bitter'. Within a few months, Gorky's stories were appearing in the prestige 'Moscow News', and in

February 1895 he joined the 'Samara Gazette' as a columnist. There he met and married a proof-reader, Yekaterina Volzhina, and in 1897, following the birth of their son Maxim, Gorky again returned to Nizhny.

Gorky's literary fortunes now took a dramatic upturn, with the publication in Moscow of his first collection, *Sketches and Stories*. Nothing could have been further from the fashionable decadence of the Symbolists than Gorky's robust tales of tramps and outcasts, and young intellectuals received his work as a call to revolution. Indeed, his sententious prose-poem, *The Song of the Stormy Petrel*, written for the new century, became their unofficial anthem.

Gorky also published his first novel, *Foma Gordeyev*, at this time, manifesting not only his loathing of the petty bourgeois world of provincial Nizhny, but also his disillusionment with the politics of reform, and his growing conviction that the future lay with the urban working-class. Gorky dedicated the novel to Chekhov, who privately found it tedious, but the two men met in person in Yalta in March 1899, at the beginning of what would prove one of Gorky's most cherished friendships.

In December 1900, Tsarist troops crushed a student revolt in Kiev, and conscripted the alleged ringleaders into the army. Gorky joined a protest march in Kazan, and was once more arrested and briefly imprisoned. Meanwhile, his play *The Petty Bourgeois*, written at the urging of Chekhov, was already in rehearsal at the Moscow Art Theatre, though its handling by the censorship was rough in the extreme.

In February 1902, Gorky was elected to the Literature Section of the Russian Academy. When the news reached the Tsar, he forced the Academy to reverse its decision, and Chekhov resigned his own membership in protest. Gorky continued to write regardless, and his next play to be staged, *The Lower Depths*, was a spectacular triumph for the Moscow Art Theatre, whose meticulously researched portrayal of his tramps and vagrants set a benchmark for theatrical realism.

Gorky was meanwhile becoming ever more embroiled in radical politics, and in the winter of 1905, the infamous events of 'Bloody Sunday' were to determine the future course of his life. Some years previously, the Tsarist government had adopted a plan to subdue industrial unrest by creating workers' associations - trade unions without teeth, in effect - and the largest of these was headed by an Orthodox priest. On Sunday, 9 January 1905, Father Gapon led a peaceful march of St Petersburg factory workers and their families to the Winter Palace, to deliver a petition. Nicholas II refused to meet them, and Cossack troops charged the unarmed demonstrators, leaving many hundreds dead and wounded.

Gorky was involved both before and after the fact, when he published a furious denunciation of the government, which led to his imprisonment in the Peter and Paul Fortress. Following widespread condemnation, however, at home and abroad, the authorities were forced to release him on bail. Gorky used his brief sojourn in prison to some purpose, and emerged on 14 February with a new play, *Children of the Sun*, all but completed. In the autumn of that year, the Tsar was finally forced to grant a constitution, guaranteeing basic civil rights, and the charges against Gorky were dropped.

Gorky's first meeting with Lenin took place in St Petersburg, in November of that year, and although they disagreed on some fundamental issues, Gorky was becoming increasingly identified with the Bolsheviks. When the latter called a general strike a few days later in Moscow, he even helped distribute weapons to the strikers at the barricades. The government response was to call in the artillery, and the insurrection was swiftly put down. At that point, Gorky decided to flee the country.

He also had personal reasons, having now left his wife for the Moscow Art Theatre actress Maria Andreyeva, and the two travelled together, first to Germany, then to the United States, arriving in New York on 10 April 1906. Gorky's plan was to campaign against the Tsarist government's appeal for aid, in the aftermath of its disastrous war with Japan, and at the same time raise money for the Bolsheviks. In the event, he succeeded in neither. Given a hero's welcome initially, Gorky became *persona non grata* the instant it was discovered that Maria Andreyeva was not his wife, and the pair were unceremoniously ejected from their New York hotel.

Thanks to the generosity of a wealthy intellectual couple, Gorky spent the summer months in the Adirondacks, where he completed another play, *Enemies*, and his proto-Socialist Realist novel *Mother*, as well as some fiercely anti-Western essays. On 13 October 1906, he left New York for Naples, and on to the island of Capri, which was to be his home for the next seven years.

During these years, closer acquaintance with Lenin failed to resolve their differences, basically over Gorky's interest in 'God-building', a strand of left-wing thought which attempted to reconcile Marxism with Christianity, and which Lenin found repugnant. In fact, as the Russian economy entered a new period of growth, Gorky felt increasingly pessimistic about the prospects for change, and it was with mixed emotions that he returned to Russia at the end of 1913, taking advantage of Nicholas II's proclamation of an amnesty to mark three hundred years of Romanov rule.

Back in St Petersburg, Gorky devoted his energies to political journalism for the most part, as the voice of reason, too often drowned out by the turbulent events attendant on Russia's entry into the Great War. Gorky genuinely feared a return to barbarism, of the sort he had witnessed among the peasants in his youthful wanderings, and he frequently attacked the Bolsheviks in his newspaper, 'New Life', comparing them to mad scientists conducting an irresponsible experiment on the Russian people.

Lenin's response, after the October Revolution which overthrew the Tsar and put the Bolsheviks in power, was to close Gorky's newspaper down, and Gorky was eventually forced to make his peace with Lenin. Despite incurring the wrath of many intellectuals, Gorky made heroic efforts to moderate the worst excesses of the new regime, and during the Civil War which followed the Revolution, he saved the lives of hundreds of artists and writers, whose only source of income was the work Gorky provided through mammoth cultural projects like his World Literature publishing house, which commissioned the translation of over two hundred European classics.

However, Lenin was no more tolerant of dissent than Nicholas II, and Gorky viewed with dismay the growing power of the Cheka, the secret police, which was to change its name many times - OGPU, NKVD, MVD, KGB - but not its nature, or sinister purpose. For their part, the Bolshevik leadership regarded Gorky as a loose cannon, and were undoubtedly relieved when ill-health forced him to return to Italy in the spring of 1924. Gorky remained there for four years, in a sense suspended between two worlds: a committed socialist, he despised Western capitalism, and had little in common with the emigré Russians who now seemed to fill every corner of Europe. However, his decision to return to his homeland, now in the control of Lenin's successor Stalin, was not easily taken, and he required a great deal of persuading.

Stalin's motives for urging his return seem clear enough - the more brutal the regime, the greater its need of good publicity, and a Gorky within Stalin's grasp could at the very least be silenced, and might even be recruited to add his powerful voice to the sycophantic chorus. Gorky's motives are more complex - financial, no doubt, but anxiety over the future of his son Maxim, an aimless, immature alcoholic, may also have influenced him. The young Maxim's friends in high places incidentally included the secret police, one of whose agents became Gorky's personal secretary - proof, if any were needed, of the extent of Stalin's network of spies and informers.

Gorky was also vain enough to believe that he could be the bard of the revolution once more, and even guide Stalin back to the true path. Initially, Stalin took care not to disabuse him, and a key stage in the process was the official announcement by the Communist Academy in 1927, affirming Gorky's status as a great proletarian writer. Even so, Gorky held out for almost five years, making a series of visits to the Soviet Union between 1928 and 1933, when he took up permanent residence.

Stalin had baited the trap well, and Gorky was understandably flattered by the sheer number of cultural projects which Stalin now placed under his direction. However, Gorky was soon to discover that his power was illusory, and his freedom of speech drastically curtailed. The last three years of his life, spent as Stalin's 'superintendent of writers', have done untold damage to his reputation, and the nadir was reached when he was persuaded to extol the 'humanity' of the labour camp regime at Solovki, as well as Stalin's brutal collectivisation programme for agriculture. Gorky has never been forgiven for his part in all this, and Solzhenitsyn, for one, describes the Solovki episode with justifiable bitterness.

Remarkably, Gorky's own writing appears to have suffered little. His epic family saga, *The Life of Klim Sanghin*, begun in Italy, remains unfinished, but he managed to complete three new plays, as well as revising his 1910 play *Vassa Zheleznova*. Other writers fared less well, as the new Writers' Union, at whose first Congress in 1934 Gorky gave the keynote speech, rapidly became an instrument of State tyranny, though to be fair, its worst excesses in the name of Socialist Realism were committed after Gorky's death.

Gorky was a virtual prisoner for the last year of his life. The death of his son Maxim in 1934 affected him deeply, but also made him more dangerous, in Stalin's view. Gorky's secretary Kriuchkov, in the pay of the NKVD, now became his jailer, denying him all contact, especially with visitors from the West. Later, it was claimed that Maxim's death had been arranged by the NKVD chief Yagoda, who had designs on Maxim's wife Nadya. True or not, Yagoda and Kriuchkov, along with the doctors who had attended Gorky in his final illness, were charged in 1938 with conspiring to murder both Gorky and Maxim, and summarily executed.

Gorky died in Moscow on 18 June 1936, officially from influenza, and the lavish State funeral ordered by Stalin took place a few days later. Rumours persist that Stalin had also ordered the writer's death, through the novelettish device of a gift of poisoned chocolates. What is certain is that Stalin used Gorky to the bitter end, even beyond the grave, and the so-called 'Doctors' Plot' became an ever-widening circle of guilt by association, sending many thousands into the labour camps, Solzhenitsyn's 'gulag archipelago', in the worst purges of Stalin's rule.

Children of the Sun: **What Happens in the Play**

The action of the play takes place in a run-down country house, occupied by Protasov, a landowner and amateur scientist, who lives there with his wife Yelena and sister Liza, and occasional house-guests, including a veterinary surgeon, Chepurnoy, the latter's widowed sister Melania, and an artist-poet, Vaghin. There are rumours of an approaching cholera epidemic, but Protasov is obsessed with his experiments, and as the play opens, he is mixing foul-smelling chemicals, much to the annoyance of his elderly housekeeper, Antonovna. Yelena is absent, at a portrait sitting with Vaghin, and both Antonovna and Liza reproach Protasov for neglecting his wife. Antonovna also urges him to deal sternly with the local blacksmith, Yegor, for wife-beating, but when Yegor appears, Protasov proves so ineffectual that he merely succeeds in enraging him.

Yegor's loutish manner upsets Liza, who is physically frail and prone to nightmare visions of mob violence. Chepurnoy tries in vain to calm her. Chepurnoy's sister Melania then arrives, and finding Protasov alone, encourages him to discuss his dream of a radiant future for all mankind. Though she barely understands him, Melania hero-worships Protasov and begs to be allowed to help - in effect, she is declaring her love for him, but Protasov is so self-absorbed that he scarcely notices. Melania then bribes the maid Fima to spy on Yelena and Vaghin, as part of her scheme to detach Protasov from his wife. Protasov's naivety is further underlined in a scene in which the local pawnbroker, Nazar, who incidentally now owns the Protasov house, easily persuades him to part with some land, while his son Misha crudely propositions the maid Fima. Misha and Fima are equally cynical, determined to marry for money, so the attempt comes to nothing. Yegor then returns, this time very drunk, to resume his argument with Protasov.

Within the household, the atmosphere is far from harmonious. Chepurnoy and the neurotically unstable Melania treat each other with ill-concealed contempt, and when Liza rebukes Chepurnoy for his harshness towards his sister, he confesses to a generally cynical outlook on life. He then proposes marriage to Liza, but receives his customary refusal. Later, Melania goes into raptures about Protasov, and his inspiring vision, but when Yelena and her artist-admirer at last return from their portrait sitting, Vaghin gives a very different picture of him, and declares his own love for her. Yelena does not respond, but as if to endorse Vaghin's view, when Protasov does appear, his only concern is for a spoiled experiment.

At the beginning of Act II, Chepurnoy expands on his gloomy view of life to Liza, and again proposes marriage, but Liza, though she evidently loves him, sees her chronic ill-health as a barrier to any happiness. Yelena, Protasov and Vaghin arrive, deep in philosophical discussion, and Yelena describes her vision of a painting in which a group of pioneers stand at the prow of a ship, sailing boldly through a violent storm, towards true humanity. The spell is broken, however, by the entry of a drunken vagrant, Troshin, seeking to renew his acquaintance with the blacksmith Yegor, and Protasov sardonically observes that Yelena's ship will have its share of barnacles. Liza is upset by this, and leaves the room. Vaghin and Protasov then develop Yelena's image further, each by his own lights – Protasov's ship will head towards the sun, the source of all life, while Vaghin's is driven on by his love for Yelena.

Protasov may be unaware of it, but the intimacy between Vaghin and Yelena has not gone unremarked by others, notably Melania, who begs Yelena to leave her husband, so that she can give Protasov the selfless devotion his genius demands, including placing her considerable fortune at his disposal. Later, in a reprise of their earlier debate, Protasov counters Liza's pessimistic view of human nature with an eloquent speech on the potential of mankind for greatness, identifying people like themselves, liberal intellectuals, as the 'children of the sun' who will lead the race out of darkness. Liza yearns desperately to believe him, but the poem she recites, in which she compares herself to a blind mole, reveals her true feelings. Vaghin responds with a poem of his own, however, which briefly restores the mood of optimism, until it is shattered by the entry of Yegor's wife Avdotia, pursued by her drunken husband and Troshin. Chepurnoy manages to outface the pair, and prevent violence, but Liza is terrified, and rushes out in hysterics.

Act III opens with Liza unburdening herself to Yelena on her fears for the future, and her feelings of isolation. Nazar then arrives to warn the family of growing concern among the villagers about a local outbreak of cholera, and a rumoured connection with Protasov's chemical experiments. Yelena testily dismisses him, but Yegor soon follows, and begs Yelena to visit his sick wife, whose symptoms sound ominously like those of the dreaded disease. Yelena agrees to do so, despite Protasov's objections, and leaves for the village. In her absence, Melania seizes her opportunity and literally throws herself at Protasov's feet. In an impassioned declaration of love, she offers to become his virtual slave, in order to advance his great work. Protasov is flattered, and tempted, but naively tells her that he will have to consult Yelena. Melania is crushed, and on Yelena's return from the village, the two women discuss Protasov's seeming lack of any real human emotion. When Protasov next appears, Melania, bowing to the inevitable, withdraws her offer, and they agree to remain friends.

Meanwhile, despite their feelings for each other, Liza finally rejects Chepurnoy's offer of marriage, and he decides to leave, masking his despondency, as ever, with some rather bleak humour. Protasov then tells Yelena about Melania's proposal, but in such a crass and insensitive way that so far from valuing his honesty, she is repelled by it. Later, Protasov is astonished when Vaghin announces that he is in love with Yelena, and when Protasov calls Yelena to hear this latest absurdity, he is even more shocked to learn that she is seriously contemplating leaving him. Protasov's self-centred reaction to this strengthens her resolve, but as he urges her to reconsider, Liza suddenly rushes into the room, crying out in terror, stricken by some strange premonition.

Act IV begins in relative calm, with Protasov reflecting complacently on his relationship with Yelena. Liza's experience of the night before has convinced her that her future lies with Chepurnoy, and she now regrets having rejected him. To make matters worse, Nazar brings news of unrest among the villagers, whose frustration at the helplessness of the medical profession against the cholera epidemic has turned to violence, and Liza grows anxious for Chepurnoy's safety. Nazar's bumptious son Misha next arrives, and manages to offend Protasov by offering him paid employment in the chemical factory he plans to build. Melania then engages Yelena in an emotional discussion about her attempt to 'buy' Protasov - she confesses her shame, but also her gratitude to Yelena, who has treated her throughout with genuine compassion. Yelena's emotions are put under further strain by the arrival of Vaghin, who accuses her of having used him to make Protasov jealous. Yelena rejects the charge, and accuses Vaghin in turn of self-interest. Vaghin insists on the sincerity of his love for her, but Yelena is unable to reciprocate.

Liza's mental state is increasingly causing concern, and when Vaghin receives a letter from Chepurnoy, which appears to be a suicide note, it is the final blow to her sanity. The egregious Misha rushes in to announce that Chepurnoy has indeed hanged himself, and Liza, tortured with guilt, has to be dragged screaming indoors. Outside the yard meanwhile, a riotous mob of villagers has assembled, in pursuit of a terrified local doctor, seeking sanctuary in the house. Led by the blacksmith Yegor, whose much-abused wife has died of cholera, despite Yelena's attentions, they break in, and make to attack Protasov. Protasov's watchman Roman vigorously comes to his defence, as does Yelena, who fires a pistol at Yegor. Yegor falls to the ground, and it appears at first as if Yelena has killed him. However, he has only been knocked out, by a blow to the head from Roman, and the fracas ends without bloodshed. Protasov then tries to make peace with Yegor, but is rudely rebuffed, experiencing yet another setback to his naive faith in the future of mankind. In the final scene, Liza enters in a trance, reminiscent of the tragic Ophelia, her mind now beyond reach, and recites a deeply pessimistic poem, the last sardonic comment on Protasov's 'children of the sun'.

The Moscow Art Theatre

The Moscow Art Theatre, founded in 1898, was the creation of Konstantin Stanislavsky and Vladimir Nemirovich-Danchenko. Stanislavsky, a wealthy merchant's son, directed and performed in his own amateur theatre company, and Nemirovich-Danchenko taught drama at the Moscow Philharmonic School, where his students included Olga Knipper, who later became Chekhov's wife, and the gifted future director Vsevolod Meyerhold.

Stanislavsky's legacy to acting, later to be known as the 'Method', placed the emphasis on psychological realism, encouraging the actor to seek an inner truth, and promoting an ideal of harmonious ensemble playing, in contrast with the then dominant 'star system'. Stanislavsky's attention to detail extended to every aspect of theatre - scenery, costumes, lighting, music and sound effects - even the colour of the curtain. Nemirovich-Danchenko shared Stanislavsky's dissatisfaction with the Russian theatre of the day, its bombastic acting and poor technical standards, and the Moscow Art Theatre duly opened in 1898 with a production of Alexei Tolstoy's historical drama *Tsar Fyodor*, notable for its opulent setting, but also its believably human characterisations.

Nemirovich-Danchenko was responsible for the repertoire, which was to be selected on literary merit alone, and the Moscow Art Theatre's place in history was assured later that same year, with the inspired choice of Chekhov's *The Seagull*. What Chekhov's plays needed - natural, unforced speaking, even-handed ensemble play-ing and exhaustive rehearsal - was perfectly expressed in the Moscow Art Theatre, and the production was a phenomenal success.

It was of course a revival, since *The Seagull* had been premièred at the Alexandrinsky Theatre in St Petersburg in 1896, when its abysmal failure had served to highlight everything that was wrong with mainstream Russian theatre. Chekhov had indeed vowed to have no more dealings with the theatre, and it may be said that Stanislavsky and Nemirovich-Danchenko rescued Chekhov the dramatist for the world, while his plays, including the two he specifically created for the Moscow Art Theatre, *Three Sisters* and *The Cherry Orchard*, gave them the perfect vehicle for their unique talents. To mark that contribution, the company adopted a seagull as its emblem, and added Chekhov's name to its official title, after his death in 1904.

Interestingly, in 1932, as part of the same process which saw Nizhny Novgorod renamed in Gorky's honour, the Moscow Art Theatre replaced Chekhov's name with that of Gorky, causing him some embarrassment. Gorky idolised Chekhov, and the crucial event in his own career as a dramatist was an invitation by Chekhov in 1900, to visit the Moscow Art Theatre on tour in the Crimea, where they performed *The Seagull* and *Uncle Vanya*. Gorky was captivated, and Chekhov urged him to try his hand at writing a play for the company, whose style he thought admirably suited to Gorky's gritty realism. Gorky needed little persuasion, and a draft of *The Lower Depths* was the result, swiftly followed by *The Petty Bourgeois*. Their relationship was not always a smooth one, however, and it is significant that after *Children of the Sun* in 1905, the company did not perform another Gorky play until his final return to the Soviet Union, in 1933. Nonetheless, his debt to the Moscow Art Theatre, like Chekhov's, is incalculable; it may indeed be argued that they made Gorky a playwright, giving him both a voice, and a fitting vehicle.

Gorky the Dramatist

Gorky's dramatic output is considerable, some fifteen full-length plays, though relatively few, among them *The Lower Depths* (1902), *Vassa Zheleznova* (1910), and *Yegor Bulychov and Others* (1931), have securely established themselves in the Russian repertoire. Remarkably, his first essay in the form, *The Lower Depths*, would go on to become his most famous achievement in any medium, but it was staged after what was in fact his second play, *The Petty Bourgeois*, which the Moscow Art Theatre chose for his theatrical debut in St Petersburg in March 1902.

From the authorities' point of view, the play was dangerously subversive, with its thinly veiled contempt for the middle-class establishment and call for revolutionary action, in the person of its proletarian hero. Accordingly, it was passed by the Tsarist censorship for four performances only, to restricted audiences, and the theatre itself was ringed by police. In the event, *The Petty Bourgeois* was not a great success, but by the time of its Moscow première that same autumn, Gorky was in exile in remote Arzamas, using his enforced leisure to re-write *The Lower Depths*, which opened at the Moscow Art Theatre on 18 December 1902.

The spectacular triumph of *The Lower Depths* took everyone by surprise, not least the government, who were driven to ban the play from working-class theatres, fearing it would incite riot. Within months it was being performed all over the world, and in published form it had sold 35,000 copies by the end of the year. Yet it is in many ways a flawed play, rambling and episodic, its semi-allegorical figures often caught up in an exchange of monologues, a technique Gorky perhaps learned from Chekhov, without Chekhov's arrow-straight sense of purpose and economy. Its central characters, the wandering sage Luka, purveyor of the Beautiful Lie, and the ex-convict Satin, cynical upholder of truth at all costs, brilliantly performed by Stanislavsky himself, together embody the ambiguity at its core, which reflects Gorky's own divided soul, and undoubtedly gives the play its power.

Chekhov exerts a more direct influence on Gorky's next play, *Summerfolk* (1903), which is clearly modelled on *The Cherry Orchard*, and is the first of four plays expressing Gorky's disillusionment with the liberal intelligentsia. Throughout these plays, which include *Children of the Sun* (1905), *Barbarians* (1906), and *Enemies* (1906), Gorky presents an effete class of privileged, well-educated people, who talk eloquently about the need for change, but are either powerless or unwilling to effect it. Strangely, given the success of *The Lower Depths*, Stanislavsky and Nemirovich-Danchenko demurred over accepting *Summerfolk* - too close to home, perhaps - and it was first produced by Vera Komissarzhevskaya's company in St Petersburg in November

1904. By all accounts, Komissarzhevskaya took a tough line with Gorky's feckless intellectuals, and *Summerfolk* was received by many as a political declaration of intent, aligning Gorky with the Social Democrats.

That remains its weakness, and in that respect, *Children of the Sun* (1905) is much more even-handed, though the gulf between the privileged lotus-eaters, and the brutish 'dark masses' whose labours sustain their life of ease, is wider still. There is no proletarian 'positive hero' to direct audience sympathies, however, and the class divisions are blurred by the presence of genuinely sensitive, caring individuals among the intelligentsia. *Children of the Sun* was premièred by Komissarzhevskaya in St Petersburg, on 12 October 1905, though the Moscow Art Theatre also staged it a few days later.

Barbarians, written more or less concurrently with *Children of the Sun*, and set in a provincial town resembling Arzamas, Gorky's place of exile in 1902, takes as its theme the conflict between Russia's agricultural and mercantile economy, and modern industrial capitalism, but its large cast of now-familiar types excited little interest from either of Gorky's main theatres, although it was premièred in Riga, in March 1906, and enjoyed some limited success in the provinces.

Following his involvement in the Moscow insurrection of December 1905, Gorky was forced to leave Russia, and his next play, *Enemies* (1906), was written at his American friends' summer house in upstate New York. Distance scarcely lent enchantment to Gorky's view, and its open declaration of class war had his sterner critics suggesting that his career as a dramatist was over, and that he was now a mere mouthpiece for the Marxists. The play's near-documentary nature, moreover, based as it was on recent incidents of violent industrial unrest, guaranteed it would be banned by the censorship, and *Enemies* was not in fact performed in Russia until 1933.

Gorky continued to write for the theatre, even in exile, and his next play, *The Last Ones* (1908), also fell foul of the censorship, because of its unflattering portrayal of the Tsarist police. Interestingly, among the plays of Gorky's last years, *Somov and Others* (1931), which treats of the infamous 1929 show trials of alleged industrial saboteurs, is now regarded as tainted by Gorky's praise of the keen-eyed hawks of the OGPU, Stalin's secret police.

At this point in his career, however, the focus of Gorky's drama shifts away from the intelligentsia, to the provincial merchant class, that dark power in the land, with their acquisitiveness and dynastic ambition, so well documented in the plays of Ostrovsky, over half a century earlier. The outstanding play of this phase is *Vassa Zheleznova* (1910), and though it received only one performance in Moscow, it was awarded the Griboyedov Prize by the Society of Russian Dramatists. Its heady mix of greed, jealousy and murder, centred on the efforts of a ruthless widow to secure her family's future at all costs, gripped Gorky's imagination sufficiently for him to re-write it in 1935, soon after the Moscow Art Theatre had begun rehearsing the original script. Between the two versions, Socialist Realism had taken root in Russian culture, a process to which Gorky had largely contributed, and it is no surprise that the revised *Vassa Zheleznova* embodies a clearer message, including a new character, Vassa's daughter-in-law, a revolutionary socialist.

Gorky returned from exile at the beginning of 1914, to become immediately embroiled in the political turmoil preceding Russia's entry into the war. As a pacifist, Gorky naturally opposed Russia's involvement, but his attitude was very different from the defeatist stance adopted by the Bolsheviks, and when the Treaty of Brest-Litovsk finally took Russia out of the war, Gorky was among those who saw it as a shameful betrayal. Gorky's polemical energies were better expressed in his journalism, however, and his plays of the Soviet period deal only rarely with the issues of the day.

Gorky was also out of touch with formal developments in the theatre, and in this respect it is interesting that as early as 1901, Chekhov had criticised *The Petty Bourgeois* for being old-fashioned. The innovations of directors like Tairov and Meyerhold thus passed Gorky by, as had those of the Symbolists earlier in his career. *The Zykovs* (1914) and *The Old Man* (1919) were staged in Petrograd, soon after the beginning of the Civil War, but neither was particularly successful, and Gorky's sojourn in the theatrical wilderness continued throughout the Soviet period, with the exception of the ever-popular *Lower Depths*, until the early 1930's.

Ironically, while the reactionary return to 'realism' in all the arts worked to Gorky's advantage, his last great play, *Yegor Bulychov and Others* (1932), owes much of its power to its symbolism. On the surface, it is a retrospective work, and the slow process of Bulychov's death from cancer takes place in the context of February 1917, the first stirrings of the revolution which will sweep away not only his mercantile empire, the timber business on which he has built his fortune, but also his entire world. Surrounded by his rapacious family, however, Bulychov is almost ready to welcome the revolution, but at the same time regrets the destruction of everything he has created. The theme of betrayal is prominent in Gorky's later work, and nowhere more so than in *Yegor Bulychov and Others*, where his true subject is perhaps Stalin's perversion of the ideals Gorky tried unsuccessfully to sustain.

Dostigaev and Others (1933) may be seen as a sequel of sorts, dealing as it does with the disintegration of a bourgeois family following the Bolshevik revolution, but it lacks the powerful characterisation of the earlier play. Finally, in addition to *Vassa Zheleznova*, Gorky also reworked *The Zykovs*, and *The Last Ones*, from the period of his exile on Capri. Thematically, his concerns are the familiar death of idealism, and the efforts of good men to keep the faith, but *The Zykovs* is noteworthy for what appears to be an oblique portrayal of Stalin, in the guise of a vicious estate manager.

Gorky's writing for the theatre is so bound up with the political events of his day, that is almost impossible to judge it fairly as drama, and indeed, any defence based on his commitment to the social purpose of art nowadays sounds like special pleading. However, in Gorky's best plays, the power of his characterisation, and the vigour of his dialogue more than compensate for an occasionally uncertain grasp of structure, and an urge to instruct, while the contradictions of his personality emerge as fascinating ambiguity, challenging audience and performers alike.

Children of the Sun

Children of the Sun, Gorky's fourth play, created in the 'romantic' setting of a prison cell in the Peter and Paul Fortress, reportedly took a mere eight days to write, and it may be that his enforced removal from the aftermath of Bloody Sunday was the best thing that could have happened to him. Certainly, compared with the later Soviet regime's treatment of its dissident voices, it is small wonder that the image of Gorky, scribbling away in monastic solitude, with the prison governor's blessing, provokes Solzhenitsyn to his most withering sarcasm.

Gorky had in fact been planning the play for some time, originally as a collaborative effort with his writer-friend Leonid Andreyev. Both had been captivated by a recently published German novel, in which an astronomer is so wrapped up in his observation of the heavens that he is oblivious to the plight of his earth-bound fellow humans, and the stirrings of revolution virtually under his feet.

In the event, the proposed collaboration fell through, and while Andreyev went on to develop the theme in his own play, *To the Stars* (1905), Gorky's version replaces the astronomer with a dilettante chemist-cum-eugenicist, and adds the complication of a cholera epidemic. Gorky's first-hand experience of politically-led violence, moreover, from the murderous peasant mobs of his days with the People's Right activists, to the professional savagery of Nicholas II's Cossacks, is reflected not only in the riot which climaxes the action, but also throughout, in Liza's blood-drenched imaginings.

Curiously, despite Gorky's seeming lack of interest in the then-fashionable Symbolist tendency in literature, *Children of the Sun* is rich in symbolic reference - storm-tossed ships, soaring eagles, blind moles, the ubiquitous sun, of course, subjected to varied interpretations, as the demands of the play, or the psychological make-up of individuals determine. The intelligentsia, routinely Gorky's target at this time, are treated more sympathetically, and the cholera epidemic, on one level a metaphor for the sickness of Russian society, also serves to illustrate their helplessness, rather than callous unconcern for the suffering villagers.

Overall, indeed, Gorky employs a lighter touch in *Children of the Sun*, and it is worth noting that he first sought the prison governor's permission to write a 'comedy'. Protasov, around whom the play revolves, is an engagingly feckless creature, the very type of the 'absent-minded professor', yet he is the main vehicle for Gorky's serious proposition that the intelligentsia, blinded by self-interest, are incapable even of communicating with the lower orders, let alone radically improving their lives. The same might be said of the artist Vaghin, for different reasons, but his own suffering, his unrequited love for Yelena, disqualifies him as an easy villain.

Gorky's strongest condemnation, in fact, is directed at the brutish peasantry, in the person of the wife-beating blacksmith Yegor, and in this play there is no proletarian 'positive hero' to complete the equation. Yegor's malevolent force, however, is somewhat diminished when the Protasovs' watchman knocks him cold with a handy plank, in the untidy fracas which eventually passes for peasant insurrection. In this context, Liza's bloody visions remain in the realm of ideas, and the play's only actual tragic events, if one omits Liza's descent into madness, are the death of Yegor's wife from cholera, and Chepurnoy's suicide, which take place well off-stage.

That is perhaps the reason for the play's fitful theatrical history, and Gorky himself regarded it as a failure. Its lack of ideological clarity, however, might be regarded as a virtue, and its flaws are mainly structural: Chepurnoy's suicide is clumsily prepared, and even although *Children of the Sun* deploys a smaller cast than many of Gorky's plays, the potentially important roles of Chepurnoy and Liza seem curiously peripheral. Protasov, for all his dazzling rhetoric, is fundamentally shallow, which to a degree blunts his message. Nonetheless, the phenomenon of the spellbinding orator, undermined by character flaws, is a mainstay of Chekhovian drama, and Protasov has something of the exasperating charm of Vershinin in *Three Sisters*, say, or Uncle Vanya. The triangular relationship of Protasov, Yelena, and Vaghin, moreover, is clearly indebted to Turgenev's *A Month in the Country*, and ideology is here secondary to the permanent human concerns of the characters, their several needs and desires.

This no doubt gave its first interpreters a few headaches, but they were as nothing compared with the problems created by the circumstances of the play's production. Expectations, in the wake of Vera Komissarzhevskaya's controversial *Summerfolk* of the previous autumn, were running high, and her proposal to stage *Children of the Sun* in April 1905 was initially blocked by the censorship. Gorky was then approached by the Moscow Art Theatre, and persuaded to allow both companies to perform the play, more or less concurrently, in St Petersburg and Moscow. Komissarzhevskaya's première thus took place in St Petersburg on 12 October, 1905, and the Moscow Art Theatre's a few days later.

Komissarzhevskaya again stressed Gorky's satire, while the Moscow Art Theatre gave more weight to the play's genuine lyricism, but it was the Moscow première that generated most excitement. As it turned out, a Bolshevik friend of the leading actor had been murdered by right-wing extremists the week before, and it was rumoured that further violence was being planned against the theatre. Accordingly, when the angry mob was heard off-stage in Act IV, many in the audience believed it to be genuine, and rushed to the exits. Nemirovich-Danchenko had to halt the performance, in an attempt to restore order, but the actors eventually took their bows to a half-empty auditorium.

Compared with what was taking place outside in the streets, *Children of the Sun* was in fact rather tame, and while it prompted some fierce debate at the time, its propaganda value diminished as attitudes steadily hardened. Its lasting value, as one of Gorky's most engaging and accessible plays, is another matter, and *Children of the Sun* is rich in incident and character, moving and funny by turns, and refreshingly free of dogma. Though it is difficult to believe that it was Gorky's conscious intention, *Children of the Sun* is perhaps best viewed as a kind of elegy - an expression, however tentative, of Gorky's regret over the failure of the Russian intelligentsia, custodians of the nation's culture, to seize the historical moment and seek a true understanding with the oppressed masses. In a few years' time, there would be no place even for regret.

The Translation

Better perhaps than any other Russian writer, Gorky knew his fellow-countrymen, and his rise through the ranks from penniless vagrant to literary stardom brought him in contact with a wide range of regional dialects and social classes. Gorky's ear for the spoken language is accordingly one of his strengths, and *Children of the Sun* demonstrates this in a number of ways. While most of the educated characters speak standard Russian, our attention is particularly drawn to Chepurnoy's Ukrainian accent, and the speech of the lower class characters ranges from the non-standard Russian of the housekeeper Antonovna, and the maid Lusha, for example, to the mixed modes of such as Troshin and Misha, whose absurd attempts to ape the manners of their superiors are reflected in their utterance. Generally, I have tried to indicate these distinctions through syntax, rather than lexis. A rare exception would be Troshin's use of 'childer' for 'children' in Act III, but in the main I have avoided non-standard spellings, which might suggest any specific dialect of English, preferring to leave that to the discretion of the director. For ease of playing, I have also for the most part simplified the Russian polite mode of address, i.e., first name and patronymic, which English speakers sometimes find difficult. A guide to pronunciation follows the play.

Stephen Mulrine

For Further Reading

The three volumes of Gorky's autobiography, *My Childhood*, *My Apprenticeship*, and *My Universities*, published as Penguin Classics in the 1970's, and regularly reprinted, rank among the great achievements in the genre, and should be read for sheer pleasure, although the story unfortunately comes to a halt in 1888, when Gorky was just twenty. For a more general account of Gorky's life and work, enlivened by some perceptive commentary, Dan Levin's *Stormy Petrel*, Frederick Muller, 1965, is still worth reading, as is the estimable Henri Troyat's *Gorky*, published in paperback by Allison & Busby, 1991. *Maxim Gorky the Writer*, by F.M.Borras, Clarendon Press, Oxford, 1967, contains a full chronology and list of works, as well as an interesting chapter on Gorky's plays, albeit not including *Children of the Sun*, though the latter is discussed at length in the collection *Fifty Years On: Gorky and his Time*, edited by Nicholas Luker, Astra Press, Nottingham, 1987. Finally, Gorky's position at the heart of Russian life and literature for almost half a century has ensured a fascinating variety of correspondents and memoirists, and these are represented in *Gorky and his Contemporaries*, Progress Publishers, Moscow, 1989, and *Maksim Gorky: Selected Letters*, ed. Andrew Barratt and Barry P Scherr, Clarendon Press, Oxford, 1997, which also has a useful biography.

Gorky: Key Dates

1868   Born Alexei Maximovich Peshkov in Nizhny Novgorod on the Volga, two hundred miles east of Moscow.

1871   Family moves to Astrakhan, where his father dies of cholera. Mother returns to Nizhny, leaves Gorky in the care of his grandmother.

1879   Mother dies of tuberculosis. At age eleven, Gorky sent from grandfather's house to earn his own living at a variety of menial jobs.

1884   Unsuccessfully attempts to enter Kazan University. While working in a bakery, becomes involved in revolutionary politics.

1887   Death of both grandparents. Gorky tries to commit suicide, fails, 12 December.

1888   Travels on foot through South Russia, works in Caspian Sea fishery, then as railway watchman on railway. Arrested for subversive activities.

1889   Plans to set up agricultural commune on Tolstoyan principles, seeks Tolstoy's aid without success.

1891   A second South Russian odyssey, through the Ukraine, Crimea and Caucasus, to Georgia.

1892   First short story, *Makar Chudra*, published in Tiflis newspaper, under pen-name 'Maxim Gorky' ('Maxim the bitter'). Returns to Nizhny with common-law wife, Olga Kaminskaya. Continues to write, poetry and short stories.

1895   Separates from Olga, moves to Samara to work as journalist. *Chelkash* published in prestige Moscow periodical.

1896   Marries Yekaterina Volzhina, newspaper proof-reader and political radical. Contracts tuberculosis, moves to Crimea for health reasons.

1897   Son Maxim born, 27 July.

1898   Arrested in Tiflis, briefly imprisoned. Two-volume *Stories and Sketches* published in St Petersburg, instant success.

1899   Meets Chekhov in Yalta. Becomes literary editor of Marxist journal 'Life'. First novel, *Foma Gordeyev*, published.

1900   Meets Tolstoy in Moscow. Introduced by Chekhov to Moscow Art Theatre in Yalta, begins work on first plays, *The Lower Depths* and *The Petty Bourgeois*.

1901   Takes part in student demonstration in St Petersburg. Imprisoned in Nizhny. Daughter Yekaterina born, 26 May. Novel *The Three* published.

1902   Gorky's election to Russian Academy of Sciences is overturned by Tsar Nicholas II. Chekhov resigns own membership in protest. *The Petty Bourgeois* premièred by Moscow Art Theatre in St Petersburg, 26 March. *The Lower Depths* premièred in Moscow, 18 December, to great acclaim.

1903   Leaves wife Yekaterina for Moscow Art Theatre actress Maria Andreyeva.

1904   Première of *Summerfolk*, 10 November, in St Petersburg.

1905   Gorky involved in organising protest march, which results in the Bloody Sunday massacre in St Petersburg, 9 January. Arrested and imprisoned in Peter and Paul Fortress, completes *Children of the Sun*. Released on bail.

Première of *Children of the Sun*, St Petersburg, 12 October; staged at the Moscow Art Theatre a few days later. First meeting with Lenin, 27 November.

1906   Involved in Moscow armed uprising, forced to flee Russia, accompanied by Maria Andreyeva. Arrives in New York, 10 April, campaigns on behalf of Bolsheviks. Newspaper furore over his extra-marital relationship with Andreyeva. Completes novel *Mother*, and play *Enemies*. Daughter Yekaterina dies of meningitis. Leaves United States for Italy, 13 October, settles in Capri.

1908   Lenin visits Gorky on Capri.

1911   Première of *Vassa Zheleznova*, February, Nezlobin Theatre, Moscow.

1913   Publishes *My Childhood*, first volume of autobiographical trilogy. Tsar decrees amnesty for political exiles, Gorky returns to St Petersburg, 31 December.

1915   Launches literary journal, 'The Chronicle'. Second volume of autobiography, *My Apprenticeship*, serialised in 'Russian Word'.

1917   Founds and edits newspaper 'New Life', frequently critical of Lenin, both before and after October Revolution.

1918   'New Life' closed down by Bolsheviks. Première of *The Zykovs* in Petrograd.

1919   Throughout Civil War, Gorky sets up various projects to assist writers and artists.

1921   Leaves Russia, to travel in Europe. Completes third volume of autobiography, *My Universities*.

1924   Death of Lenin, 21 January. Gorky settles in Sorrento.

1927   Communist Academy declares Gorky 'a proletarian writer', 22 October.

1928	Returns to Russia, first in series of lengthy visits, 28 May.
1930	Begins work on trilogy of plays, *Somov and Others*, *Yegor Bulychov and Others*, and *Dostigaev and Others*.
1932	Gorky's fortieth anniversary as a writer, 17 September. Awarded Order of Lenin, and Nizhny Novgorod renamed Gorky.
1933	Settles permanently in USSR.
1934	Death of son Maxim, 11 May. Gorky elected Chairman of First All-Union Congress of Soviet Writers, August-September.
1935	Applies for permission to travel abroad, refused.
1936	Dies 18 June, Moscow, in suspicious circumstances.

Guide to Pronunciation of Names

Where the stress in English polysyllables tends to fall on the penultimate syllable, Russian stress, which is also heavier, is less predictable, and this gives rise to pronunciation difficulties, quite apart from its unfamiliar consonant clusters. The following is an approximation of those names and places which might present difficulty in the spoken text, with the stressed syllables marked in capitals:

Antonovna	Ahn-TOH-nov-nah
Avdeyich	Ahv-DAY-itch
Avdotia	Ahv-DOH-tee-yah
Boris	Baw-REES
Chepurnoy	Cheh-POOR-noy
Dmitri	DMEE-tree
Fima	FEE-mah
Fyodorych	FYAW-daw-ritch
Kaluga	Kah-LOO-gah
Kazan	Kah-ZAHN
Khrapov	KHRAH-poff ('kh' as 'ch' in Scottish 'loch')
Kocherin	KOH-cher-een ('ch' as in 'chair')
Lena	LAY-nah
Lizaveta	Lee-zah-VYAY-tah
Lukeriya	Loo-KAY-ree-yah
Lusha	LOO-shah
Melania	Meh-LAH-nee-yah
Mikhail	Mee-khy-EEL ('kh' as 'ch' in Scottish 'loch')
Misha	MEE-shah
Mogilev	Moh-geel-YOFF (hard 'g')
Nazar	NAH-zar

Nazarovich	Nah-ZAH-roh-vitch
Nikolaevich	Nee-koh-LIE-yeh-vitch
Nikolaevna	Nee-koh-LIE-yehv-nah
Pavel	PAH-vel
Poltava	Pawl-TAH-vah
Protasov	Proh-TAH-soff
Ryazan	Ryah-ZAHN (two syllables)
Sergeyevich	Ser-GAY-yeh-vitch
Yelena	Yeh-LAY-nah
Roman	Roh-MAN
Troshin	TROH-sheen
Vaghin	VAH-geen (hard 'g')
Yakov	YAH-koff
Yaroslavl	Yah-roh-SLAHVL
Yegor	YEH-gor
Zotikov	ZOH-tee-koff

CHILDREN OF THE SUN

Dramatis Personae

PROTASOV, Pavel Fyodorovich
LIZA, *his sister*
YELENA NIKOLAEVNA, *his wife*
VAGHIN, Dmitri Sergeyevich
CHEPURNOY, Boris Nikolaevich
MELANIA, *his sister*
NAZAR AVDEYEVICH
MISHA, *his son*
YEGOR, *a smith*
AVDOTIA, *his wife*
YAKOV TROSHIN
ANTONOVNA, *an old nurse*
FIMA, *a maid*
LUSHA, *a maid*
ROMAN
A Doctor

Act One

The scene is an old country house. A large, shady room; to the left, a window and a door, giving out onto the terrace; a staircase in the corner, leading up to LIZA's room; up-stage, an arch, and beyond it the dining-room; to the right, a doorway to YELENA's room. Bookcases, solid antique furniture, expensive editions of books on the tables, portraits of scientists on the walls. A white bust on top of a cupboard. By the stage left window is a large round table, at which sits PROTASOV, leafing through a pamphlet and watching a retort with some liquid in it, heating up over a spirit lamp. ROMAN is pottering about on the terrace under the window, singing in a dreary monotone. PROTASOV is disturbed by his singing.

PROTASOV. Excuse me! I say, excuse me!

ROMAN (*at the window*). What?

PROTASOV. Um . . . would you mind going away, please?

ROMAN. Where to?

PROTASOV. Well . . . anywhere. You're putting me off my work.

ROMAN. But the landlord told me . . . he said I was to fix this.

ANTONOVNA (*entering from the dining-room*). Heavens, what a messy creature! You've come in here now with your . . .

PROTASOV. Oh, Nanny, do be quiet.

ANTONOVNA. As if you haven't got enough space in your own rooms . . .

PROTASOV. Nanny, please don't go in there – I've been fumigating the place.

ANTONOVNA. Yes, and now you'll be making fumes in here. At least let me open the door.

PROTASOV (*hastily*) No, no, please don't! Oh, really, Nanny – look, I'm not asking you . . . Just tell the watchman to go away. He's mooing like a cow .

ANTONOVNA (*through the window*). Hey, Roman! What are you doing out there? Go away!

ROMAN. What d'you mean? Nazar Avdeyich told me to . . .

ANTONOVNA. Go on, clear off! You can see to that later.

ROMAN. Oh, all right then. (*Goes off, making a clattering noise.*)

ANTONOVNA (*grumbling*). You know, you'll suffocate yourself one of these days. And there's supposed to be cholera on the way. A general's son you may be, but God knows what you're up to, all you do is make nasty smells.

PROTASOV. You wait and see, Nanny, I'll be a general too.

ANTONOVNA. You'll end up on the streets. You've got this house practically burnt down with your chemicals and physicals.

PROTASOV. Physics, Nanny, not physicals. Now, please, leave me in peace.

ANTONOVNA. There's someone just arrived . . . it's that Yegor.

PROTASOV. Tell him to come in.

ANTONOVNA. Now, Pasha dear, listen – you've got to speak to him, that good-for-nothing creature, you ask him what he's been up to. I tell you, he just about beat that wife of his to death again yesterday.

PROTASOV. All right, I'll speak to him.

LIZA *comes downstairs, enters unnoticed. She stands in front a bookcase, and quietly opens it.*

ANTONOVNA. Well, you give him a good talking to – you just say to him, I'll give you what for!

PROTASOV. All right, all right, I'll put the wind up him! Now don't you worry, Nanny, just go, please.

ANTONOVNA. You've got to be strict with him. And here's you talking to all the servants like they was gentlefolk . . .

PROTASOV. Nanny, that's enough, please! Is Yelena at home?

ANTONOVNA. No, not yet. She went to see that Vaghin after breakfast, and she hasn't been back. Better watch you don't lose that wife of yours.

PROTASOV. Oh, don't talk rubbish, Nanny! I'll . . . I'll lose my temper, I really shall.

LIZA. Nanny, you're keeping Pavel off his work.

PROTASOV. Oh, it's you? So, how are you?

LIZA. Fine.

ANTONOVNA. It's time for your milk, Liza dear.

LIZA. I know.

ANTONOVNA. And I'll tell you this – if I were in Yelena Nikolaevna's place I'd be off having an affair with somebody. You don't pay any attention to the woman. You've had your fun, now that's you done, eh? And you've got no children neither, what sort of life is that for a woman? I tell you, if it was me . . .

PROTASOV. Nanny! I'm starting to get angry . . . now go away! Honestly, you're like . . . you're like glue!

ANTONOVNA. Ooh . . . he's so fierce! Now don't you forget about Yegor . . . (*Makes to exit.*) Your milk's in the dining-room, Liza dear. And what about your drops, have you taken them?

LIZA. Yes, yes!

ANTONOVNA. Right, then. (*Exits to the dining-room.*)

PROTASOV (*looking round*) She really is priceless, that woman. She's like stupidity, she'll never die . . . and she's just as persistent. So, how are you feeling, Liza?

LIZA. I'm fine.

PROTASOV. Good, good – that's wonderful! (*Starts singing.*) That's wonderful, that's wonderful . . .

LIZA. You know, Nanny's right.

PROTASOV. Oh, I doubt it. Old people are very seldom right. Truth comes out of the mouths of babes, always. Liza, take a look at this – look, here I have some simple baker's yeast . . .

LIZA. Nanny's right, when she says you don't pay enough pay attention to Yelena.

PROTASOV (*mildly irritated*). Why d'you keep going on at me, you and Nanny? I mean, has Yelena lost her tongue or what? She's surely capable of telling me herself, if there's something I should . . . if there's anything not right, or if she needs . . . well, anyway . . . But she says nothing! So what's the matter?

YEGOR *emerges from the dining-room, a little drunk.*

Ah, it's Yegor! Good morning, Yegor.

YEGOR. Your good health.

PROTASOV. Well, now, Yegor . . . er, there's something I want to . . . um . . . the fact is, Yegor . . . actually, I'd like you to make a little brazier . . . with a lid . . . sort of a cone-shaped lid, and on the top of it a little round aperture, with a pipe coming out . . . You know what I mean?

YEGOR. Yes, I know. I can do that.

PROTASOV. Actually, I've got a drawing . . . now, where is it? Come with me.

He takes YEGOR *into the dining-room.* CHEPURNOY *knocks at the door leading from the terrace.* LIZA *opens it.*

CHEPURNOY. Ah, Liza, you're at home. Good morning.

LIZA. Hello.

CHEPURNOY (*wrinkling his nose*). And my colleague's at home, judging by the smell.

LIZA. Where have you been?

CHEPURNOY. On a house call, no less. The workhouse supervisor's wife got her dog's tail crushed – her maid slammed the door on it – so I bandaged up the aforesaid tail, and they gave me three roubles – look! I was going to buy you some chocolates, then I thought, well, it's a bit off, treating you out of my dog money, so I didn't bother.

LIZA. And you were quite right not to. Sit down, please.

CHEPURNOY. Hm, I must say, the stink off that . . . that soup – makes your invitation a bit dubious. (*Calls to* PROTASOV.) I think this is boiling now, my friend!

PROTASOV (*hurries out*). No, no, it mustn't boil! Oh, how could you? Why didn't you tell me?

CHEPURNOY. I've just told you it was boiling.

PROTASOV (*annoyed*). No, you don't understand – I really didn't want it to boil!

YEGOR *enters.*

LIZA. Well, who was supposed to know that, Pavel?

PROTASOV (*grumbles*). Hm . . . Oh, damn! Now I'll have to start all over again . . .

YEGOR. Pavel Fyodorych, let me have a rouble.

PROTASOV. A rouble? Oh . . . hold on . . . (*Searches through all his pockets.*) Liza, have you any money?

LIZA. No. Nanny has some.

CHEPURNOY. So have I – look, three roubles!

PROTASOV. Three? Let's have them, please. There you are, Yegor, three roubles – will that do?

YEGOR. That's fine – we'll settle up later. Thanks. Well, I'm off . . . 'bye . . .

LIZA. Pavel, Nanny asked you to have a word with him – did you forget?

PROTASOV. A word about what? Oh, yes . . . Hm . . . yes. Yegor, hold on . . . come back . . . Er . . . take a seat, please. Oh, Liza, couldn't you speak to him? (LIZA *shakes her head.*) Well, you see, Yegor . . . Um . . . I've got to tell you . . . that is, Nanny asked me to . . . well, you see, the fact is . . . I mean . . . Look, you don't really beat your wife, do you? I'm sorry to have to ask, Yegor, but . . .

YEGOR (*stands up*). Yes, I do.

PROTASOV. You do? Er . . . well, you know, that's really not good enough . . .

YEGOR (*morosely*). So what?

PROTASOV. Eh? D'you know what I'm saying? I mean, why do you do it? It's atrocious, Yegor, you've got to stop it. Heavens, man, you're a human being, you're a sentient creature, you're the most radiant, beautiful phenomenon on this earth . . .

YEGOR (*mocking*). Who, me?

PROTASOV. Yes, you.

YEGOR. Look, sir, shouldn't you have asked me first what I beat her for?

PROTASOV. No, understand me – you mustn't beat her. People shouldn't, people can't beat each other – that's absolutely clear, Yegor!

YEGOR (*with a mocking smile*). Well, I've been beaten, and more than once, too. And if it's my wife you're talking about, she's not a human being, she's a damn devil.

PROTASOV. Oh, that's rubbish. What do you mean, a devil?

YEGOR (*resolutely*). Look, I'm going . . . And I'll beat her all right . . . I'll beat her till she can't stand up, till she's bent double, like the grass in a high wind! (*Exits to the dining-room.*)

PROTASOV. Now look here, Yegor! You said yourself . . . Dammit, he's gone! And I think he's offended. This is so stupid. It's Nanny's fault, that's what it is. She's always making trouble, it's ridiculous! (*Exits through the portière, annoyed.*)

CHEPURNOY. Well, he made his point, didn't he.

LIZA. Poor, dear Pavel – he's always so funny!

CHEPURNOY. I'd take a stick to that Yegor, frankly.

LIZA. Boris Nikolaevich!

CHEPURNOY. So? Well, I'm sorry to be so blunt. But he's absolutely right: he's been beaten, so he can beat other people. And I'd go further – he needs beating again!

LIZA. Please, don't. Why are you speaking like that?

CHEPURNOY. After all, it's precisely that kind of logic that underpins any penal code.

LIZA. You know how I hate . . . how *frightened* I am by any sort of vulgarity, and you're always teasing me, it's as if you do it on purpose. No, listen . . . That blacksmith, that Yegor, he frightens me. He's so . . . so dark . . . and those huge, wounded eyes of his . . . It's as if I've seen them somewhere . . . some-time, I don't know, in a crowd of people . . .

CHEPURNOY. Oh, don't give it another thought. Forget him.

LIZA. Can you honestly forget him?

CHEPURNOY. Why not?

LIZA. Flowers don't ever grow where blood's been spilt . . .

CHEPURNOY. Oh, they grow all right, and with a vengeance!

LIZA (*stands up and begins pacing to and fro*). No, the only thing that grows there is hate. Whenever I hear anyone being rude, or off-hand, whenever I see the colour red, a kind of sick feeling of horror rises up in my heart, and I can see, right in front of my eyes, those dark masses, brutalised, their faces stained with blood, pools of warm red blood on the sand . . .

CHEPURNOY. Liza, you're going to talk yourself into a fit again.

LIZA. And at my feet, there's a young man with his head smashed in . . . he's trying to crawl somewhere, and there's blood running down his cheek and his neck, he lifts his head up to the skies . . . I can see his glazed eyes, his open mouth and his teeth stained with blood . . . and he falls face down onto the sand . . . face down . . .

CHEPURNOY (*goes up to her*). God in Heaven, Liza, what am I going to do with you!

LIZA. Doesn't that frighten you at all?

CHEPURNOY. Look, let's go into the garden.

LIZA. No, I want you to tell me: can you understand my fear?

CHEPURNOY. What do you mean? Of course I understand . . . I can feel it.

LIZA. That's not true. If you did understand, things would be easier . . . I want to shed this terrible burden, I want to cast it out of my soul, but there isn't another soul willing to accept it . . . not one!

CHEPURNOY. Mother of God! Well, go on, cast it out! And let's go into the garden, please . . . there's a fearful stink in here – it's as if somebody's been frying rubber galoshes in sunflower oil!

LIZA. Yes . . . the smell's making me giddy.

ANTONOVNA (*from the dining-room*). Liza dear! Remember to take your drops, and you still haven't drunk your milk!

LIZA (*goes into the dining-room*). In a minute . . .

CHEPURNOY. So, how are things, Antonovna?

ANTONOVNA (*clearing the table*). Oh, not bad . . . mustn't grumble . . .

CHEPURNOY. Good, good – keeping well?

ANTONOVNA. Yes, thanks be to God.

CHEPURNOY. What a shame – I'd have cured you.

ANTONOVNA. No, you do better with dogs. And I'm no dog.

LIZA *enters*.

CHEPURNOY. Still, I quite fancy treating a nice human being.

LIZA. Let's go now.

They exit onto the terrace. PROTASOV *appears, holding a flask.*

PROTASOV. Nanny, some boiling water, please.

ANTONOVNA. There isn't any.

PROTASOV. Oh, come on, Nanny – please?

ANTONOVNA. You'll have to wait till the samovar boils. Did you speak to that Yegor?

PROTASOV. Yes, I spoke to him.

ANTONOVNA. Sternly?

PROTASOV. Extremely! Actually, he was scared stiff, shaking in his boots. I told him, I said, now you look here, I'll report you to the . . . er . . . what d'you call it?

ANTONOVNA. The chief of police?

PROTASOV. No, no . . . well, anyway, it doesn't matter. Oh yes, the magistrate . . . the local magistrate . . .

ANTONOVNA. You should've tried frightening him with the police. So what did he say to that?

PROTASOV. Well, he said . . . er, he said . . . actually, he said I was a fool . . .

ANTONOVNA (*indignant*). He did what?

PROTASOV. Yes, he did. Absolutely. You're a fool, he says, it's none of your business.

ANTONOVNA. He said that? Pasha, did he really say that?

PROTASOV (*laughs*). No, of course not, Nanny. It wasn't him, that's what I said to myself. He had a think about it, and I said . . .

ANTONOVNA. Oh, you! . . . (*Makes to exit, annoyed.*)

PROTASOV. And Nanny, please bring me the boiling water yourself . . . that fashion-plate Fima's always catching something with the hem of her dress or her sleeves.

ANTONOVNA. I think that Fima of yours is up to her tricks with the landlord's son, that's what I think!

PROTASOV. What, are you jealous?

ANTONOVNA. Huh! Maybe you ought to tell her – you're the master, you tell her it's not right for young girls!

PROTASOV. Oh, for Heaven's sake, Nanny! Honestly, if you had your way, I'd be going around the whole day, telling everybody what's right and what's not right. It really isn't my business.

ANTONOVNA. So what did you get an education for? Eh?

MELANIA *appears at the terrace doors.*

PROTASOV. Look, Nanny, just go, please! Ah, it's Melania, hello!

MELANIA. Good morning, Pavel Fyodorych.

ANTONOVNA. And who forgot to lock this door! (*Locks it.*)

MELANIA. You're looking pleased with yourself!

PROTASOV. I'm pleased because you've come. Nanny's been nagging me to death. *And* I've managed to do some very interesting work today . . .

MELANIA. Really? I'm delighted to hear it. I so much want you to become famous . . .

ANTONOVNA (*exits, muttering*). Famous? Huh, he's the talk of the town already.

MELANIA. I truly believe you'll be another Pasture.

PROTASOV. Eh? Well, it's not important, but it's actually pronounced Pasteur. Is that my book? Have you read it? It's more interesting than a novel, now, isn't it? Wouldn't you agree?

MELANIA. Oh yes, it is. The only thing is, these signs . . .

PROTASOV. The formulae?

MELANIA. Yes, formulaes. I don't understand them.

PROTASOV. Well, you just have to learn them, really. I'll give you some stuff on the physiology of plants now, but first of all, and most important, you must study chemistry – yes, chemistry. That's an amazing science, you know. It's still not well developed, in comparison with the others, but I already think of it as a kind of all-seeing eye. Its bold, piercing gaze can penetrate both the fiery mass of the sun, and the darkness of the earth's core, and the invisible particles of your heart . . .

MELANIA *sighs*.

And the hidden structures of stones, and the silent life of trees. It looks everywhere, and discovering harmony in all things, it relentlessly seeks the origin of life itself. And it'll find it, yes! And once it has learned the structure of matter, it'll create a living organism in a glass jar . . .

MELANIA (*ecstatically*). Oh Lord! Why don't you give lectures?

PROTASOV (*embarrassed*). Er . . . why should I do that?

MELANIA. But you absolutely must! You speak so enchantingly . . . when I'm listening to you, I just want to kiss your hand.

PROTASOV (*inspects his hands*). Mm . . . I wouldn't advise that. Actually, my hands are very seldom clean. You know, you get them into all sorts of things . . .

MELANIA (*sincerely*). Oh, I'd love to do something for you! Oh, if only you knew! I admire you so much, you're so unworldly, so exalted. Tell me what you want. Ask anything of me, anything!

PROTASOV. Er . . . well, actually you could . . . um . . .

MELANIA. Yes, yes! What could I do?

PROTASOV. Er . . . you wouldn't happen to keep hens?

MELANIA. Hens? What d'you mean, hens?

PROTASOV. You know, domestic fowl. The chicken family – cocks, hens . . .

MELANIA. I know. Yes, I've got hens. What do you want them for?

PROTASOV. Wonderful! If you could just bring me some fresh eggs every day – absolutely fresh, new-laid eggs, still warm! You see, I need a great deal of albumen, and Nanny, well, she's a bit miserly, she doesn't understand, she doesn't know what albumen is. She gives me old, stale eggs, and I have to keep going on about it – that sour face of hers . . .

MELANIA. Oh, Pavel Fyodorych, you're so cruel!

PROTASOV. Cruel? What d'you mean?

MELANIA. Oh, never mind. I'll send you a dozen eggs every morning.

PROTASOV. Wonderful! That'll do splendidly. And I do thank you, so very much! You're an absolute darling, truly.

MELANIA. And you're a child, a cruel child! You don't understand anything.

PROTASOV (*puzzled*). Indeed I don't understand – what do you mean, cruel?

MELANIA. Oh, you'll find out, one of these days. Isn't Yelena Nikolaevna at home?

PROTASOV. No, she's at Vaghin's, at a portrait sitting.

MELANIA. Do you like him?

PROTASOV. Who, Vaghin? Oh, yes. I mean, we're old friends. We went to school together, then university. (*Looks at his watch.*) He was studying science too, but he gave up in second year, to enter the Academy.

MELANIA. Yelena Nikolaevna's fond of him too, I gather.

PROTASOV. Oh yes, extremely. He's a splendid fellow, a bit limited, perhaps.

MELANIA. And you're not afraid he . . .

CHEPURNOY *knocks at the terrace door.*

PROTASOV. Afraid of what? Nanny must have locked this. (*Unlocks the door.*)

MELANIA. Oh, you're here?

CHEPURNOY. And you're here already? Where do you keep the water? Liza's asking for some.

PROTASOV. Is she unwell?

CHEPURNOY. No, no, she's fine . . . it's to take her drops. (*Goes into the dining-room.*)

PROTASOV. Well, if you'll excuse me for a moment, Melania. I'll have to take a look at my . . .

MELANIA. Yes, yes, please go. And come back soon.

PROTASOV. Yes, of course. Why don't you go into the garden?

MELANIA. I'll do that.

PROTASOV. Liza's there. Nanny! What's happened to my water? (*Exits.*)

CHEPURNOY (*emerges*). So, Melania . . . how are things?

MELANIA (*hurriedly, sotto voce*). Listen, Boris . . . you wouldn't happen to know what hydatopyromorphism is?

CHEPURNOY. Eh?

MELANIA. Hydato . . . pyro . . . morphism?

CHEPURNOY. God knows! Probably some sort of water-firework . . .

MELANIA. You're pulling my leg.

CHEPURNOY. Well, that's what it sounds like. 'Pyro' from pyrotechnics, 'morphism' from metamorphosis, a kind of conjuring trick. What's all this about, is he giving you homework?

MELANIA. None of your business. Go away.

CHEPURNOY. Anyway, when you manage to liberate him from his wife, you should build a soap factory: you won't need to pay wages to the chemist. (*Exits to the garden.*)

MELANIA. Boris, you really are insufferable! (*Stands up, has a look round.*)

FIMA *enters.*

FIMA. Ma'am, the young mistress wants you to come out to the garden.

MELANIA. All right.

ANTONOVNA *brings on a pot of hot water.* FIMA *is rattling dishes in the dining-room.*

What's that you're carrying, Nanny?

ANTONOVNA. It's boiled water for Pasha.

MELANIA. I see, it's for his experiments.

ANTONOVNA. Oh yes, everything's for them.

MELANIA (*looks into the dining-room*). Fima!

FIMA (*appears at the door*). Yes, ma'am?

MELANIA. Does the mistress go to see the artist every day?

FIMA. No, ma'am, she doesn't go if it's raining, or cloudy. Mr Vaghin comes here instead.

MELANIA (*goes up close to her*). Fima, you're a bright girl, yes?

FIMA. I'm not stupid, ma'am.

MELANIA. Well, if you should happen to notice anything about them, you'll tell me, won't you? You understand?

FIMA. Yes, ma'am.

MELANIA. And say nothing. Here, I'll make it worth your while.

FIMA. Thank you most kindly, ma'am. Er . . . he does kiss her hand . . .

MELANIA. Hm, that's not much. Anyway, keep a look out.

FIMA. Very well, ma'am. I understand.

MELANIA. I'm going into the garden – call me when Pavel Fyodorych appears. (*Exits.*)

FIMA. Yes, ma'am.

ANTONOVNA *enters*.

ANTONOVNA. Who's that rattling the cups, as if they were tin cans? You'll smash the things.

FIMA. What, you think I don't know how to wash dishes?

ANTONOVNA. Now, don't be cheeky! What was her ladyship asking you?

FIMA (*exiting to the dining-room*). She was asking about the young mistress – how she was keeping.

ANTONOVNA (*calling after her*). Huh – you'd think she could go and see for herself, instead of badgering the servants.

NAZAR AVDEYEVICH *enters from the terrace, takes off his cap, looks round the room, sighs, runs his finger over the wallpaper with his finger, then coughs.*

FIMA (*from the dining-room*). That's where she's gone. And servants are people too. Anyway, you're a servant yourself.

ANTONOVNA. I know what I am. And real gentry don't have conversations with servants, they give orders, and that's that! Nowadays they're never away from the alehouse, and as for their manners – they're no better than beasts. Who's that?

NAZAR. It's me. Your very good health, Nanny!

ANTONOVNA. What do you want?

NAZAR. I've come to see Pavel Fyodorych. I'm to have a talk with him.

ANTONOVNA. I'll go and tell him.

FIMA (*looks out from the dining-room*). Hello, Nazar Avdeyich!

NAZAR. Yefimia, my dear, good morning! Oh, you're a crafty one, you are, a right little minx!

FIMA. I beg your pardon! Hands off, please, touching's not allowed.

NAZAR. What, you'd turn down a rich widower? A nice little drink of tea in the evening . . .

FIMA. Ssshhh . . .

PROTASOV *enters, followed by* ANTONOVNA.

PROTASOV. You've come to see me?

NAZAR. Indeed, sir.

PROTASOV. What's it about?

NAZAR. Well, it's about the rent, sir.

PROTASOV (*faintly irritated*). Now look here, when I sold you this house, I had to wait a whole two years for hundreds of roubles, and now you . . . Oh, all right – when do I have to pay?

NAZAR. Well, it should've been yesterday, sir.

PROTASOV. What! Well, honestly, this is a bit awkward. I'm busy here, and you just arrive, and so forth…

NAZAR. Actually, that's not why I've come. I just mentioned the money in passing, to remind myself, so to speak.

PROTASOV. Well, you can remind Nanny there, or my wife. There is money, but I'm damned if I know where it is. It's in a drawer somewhere, my wife'll send it to you. Or Nanny'll bring it . . . now, goodbye!

ANTONOVNA *exits to the dining-room.*

NAZAR. Sir, I won't keep you a moment.

PROTASOV. What is it? What do you want?

NAZAR. It's about that little bit of land of yours, and the cottage.

PROTASOV. What about it?

NAZAR. Well, you might want to sell it.

PROTASOV. Eh? Who in their senses would buy that? It's no use for anything – nothing but sand, and fir-trees.

NAZAR (*excitedly*). That's right, sir, you're absolutely right. The land's no good to anybody.

PROTASOV. You see? I told you.

NAZAR. And nobody but me would want to buy it.

PROTASOV. Why you?

NAZAR. Why, to make it all of a piece, sir! I've already bought your neighbour's patch. So now I'd like yours.

PROTASOV. Splendid! Go ahead and buy it then. Still making pots of money, are you?

NAZAR. Well, how can I put it, sir? I'm expanding.

PROTASOV. You know, you're really funny. I mean, what do you want with a patch of sand?

NAZAR. Ah well, you see, sir – that son of mine's finished business school now, and he's turned out a right well-educated young man. He's got all sorts of bright ideas about industry, so here's me got this urge to expand Russian industry, like. I'm thinking of setting up a little factory, to make beer bottles.

FIMA *is at the dining-room door, listening.*

PROTASOV (*chuckles*). No, you're not serious! And are you going to close down the pawnshop?

NAZAR. Now, why would I do that? No, no, the pawnshop's for the good of my soul. It's a charitable institution, sir . . . it's for the benefit of my neighbours.

PROTASOV (*laughs*). Really? Oh well, go ahead, you can buy my land. Now, goodbye! (*Exits, still laughing.*)

NAZAR. Well, thank you, sir! Eh? Where's he gone? Fima, why's he gone off like that? I mean, you need both parties to strike a deal, and he's just walked out?

FIMA (*shrugs*). Well, he's a bit touched, frankly.

NAZAR. Hmm . . . that's silly, that is. Well, I'm off anyway – 'bye! (*Exits.*)

ROMAN (*behind* FIMA). So where's this stove that's smoking?

FIMA. Oh, you! Go to blazes! What do you want?

ROMAN. What are you scared of? The stove's smoking, can't you smell it?

MISHA (*runs in from the dining-room*). It's not in here, you great lump! It's in the kitchen.

ROMAN. I thought it was in here. (*Exits.*)

MISHA (*hurriedly*). Well, Fima, what d'you say? A nice flat and fifteen roubles a month – d'you agree?

FIMA. Get off, you cheeky creature! Anybody'd think you were buying a horse!

MISHA. Well, I like that! I'm a businessman. Just think who you could be marrying – you could wind up with a common workman, who'd beat you up, yes, same as that smith of ours beats his wife. But I'll treat you decently, with a bit of respect, you'll have a good life, and what's more, I'll see to your education.

FIMA. That's enough of that – I'm an honest woman. Anyway, Khrapov the butcher's offered me a hundred roubles a month.

MISHA. Eh? But he's an old man, for God's sake! Just think about it.

FIMA. I haven't accepted him.

MISHA. Well, there you are, you silly little fool – I mean, I'd give you . . .

FIMA. Give me seventy-five.

MISHA. What! Seventy-five?

FIMA. And an IOU, for a year's money.

MISHA (*troubled*). What, you mean . . . ?

FIMA. That's right.

They gaze at each other expressively. YEGOR *enters from the terrace, thoroughly drunk.*

Ssshhh . . . Listen, your father's gone.

MISHA. Has he? I'd better go. (*Exits.*)

FIMA. So, where are you creeping off to? Couldn't you go through the kitchen? The master himself goes through the kitchen, and you . . .

YEGOR. Oh, shut up. Get me the master.

FIMA. Huh, and drunk besides! What's the master going to say to you?

YEGOR. None of your business. You get him down here! I'll do the talking. Go on!

FIMA (*runs into the dining-room*). Nanny! Nanny!

PROTASOV (*emerges from behind the portière*). What's all the shouting about, Fima? Oh, it's you, Yegor. What do you want? I'm busy, make it quick, please.

YEGOR. Now just hold on . . . I've had a little bit to drink. I can't talk when I'm sober.

PROTASOV. Yes, yes, what's the matter?

ANTONOVNA *enters from the dining-room, followed by* FIMA.

YEGOR. A while back you insulted me in front of people. You started talking about my wife. Who do you think you are, insulting me like that?

PROTASOV. You see what you've done, Nanny? Hah! Yegor, I didn't mean to offend you.

YEGOR. No, hold on . . . I've had to put up with abuse since I was a child.

PROTASOV. Well, yes, of course, Yegor, I understand that, but . . .

YEGOR. No, let me finish! Nobody likes me, nobody understands me. Not even my wife likes me. And I *want* people to like me, damn you to hell!

PROTASOV. There's no need to shout.

ANTONOVNA. Huh, pig-drunk, is he?

YEGOR. Am I a human being or not? Why does everybody insult me?

ANTONOVNA. Good God, what's going on?

She runs into the dining-room. We can hear her shouting outside.

PROTASOV. Now calm down, Yegor. Anyway, it was Nanny that told me . . .

YEGOR. You should get rid of Nanny, you're a grown man, for God's sake. Grown men don't take orders from nannies. Now you listen to me: I respect you – I can see you're a special sort of person, I can feel it . . . and well, that makes it all the more offensive, you telling me in front of people . . . Oh, for God's sake, what do you want – d'you want me to fall down on my knees in front of you? I mean, man to man, I wouldn't have minded, but in front of that damn horse-doctor. Right, then, I'll beat my wife. I'll give her a good hiding. I love her, and she owes me a bit of . . .

CHEPURNOY, MELANIA, LIZA, ANTONOVNA and FIMA *all rush in.*

LIZA. What's going on? Pavel, what is it?

CHEPURNOY (*holding* LIZA *back*). What's the matter? Well, come on?

PROTASOV. Please, leave us alone.

MELANIA. Nanny, send for the watchman!

ANTONOVNA (*exits and shouts*). Roman!

YEGOR. Huh! The carrion crows have arrived. Well, you can shoo them off right now, Pavel Fyodorych!

CHEPURNOY. Now look, be a good fellow, and get back off home, eh?

YEGOR. I'm not your good fellow . . .

CHEPURNOY (*frowning*). Just go, nevertheless!

MELANIA. We ought to call the police.

PROTASOV. No, please – that's not necessary. Yegor, go away . . . I'll come and see you later myself.

ANTONOVNA *and* ROMAN *appear in the dining-room doorway.*

YEGOR. You'll come?

PROTASOV. Yes.

YEGOR. Well, all right . . . we'll see. You're not lying?

PROTASOV. Word of honour.

YEGOR. Right! Goodbye, then. You know, all these people – they're like dirt beside you. Goodbye! (*Exits.*)

ROMAN. Does that mean I'm not needed?

PROTASOV. No. Go away. Whew! Well, Nanny, d'you see?

ANTONOVNA *sighs.*

PROTASOV. That was all your doing.

LIZA. I'm frightened of that man . . . I really am.

MELANIA. You're much too soft on him, Pavel Fyodorych.

PROTASOV. I actually felt guilty in front of him.

LIZA. You'd better get another blacksmith, Pavel.

CHEPURNOY. Workmen – they're all drunkards.

PROTASOV. Look, this is getting on my nerves, I'm worn out! I'm having no luck today at all. All kinds of stupid trivialities breaking in on me. I've got a very complicated experiment on the go, with cyanic acid, and now this. Liza, pour me some tea . . .

LIZA. I'll tell them to bring the tea through here. You don't like the dining-room. (*Exits.*)

PROTASOV. Good, fine. No, I don't like dark rooms, and there aren't any bright ones in this house.

MELANIA. Oh, I know what you mean, Pavel Fyodorych.

CHEPURNOY. Er . . . Melania, what's that word again?

MELANIA. What word?

CHEPURNOY. You know, the one you were asking about?

MELANIA. I didn't ask you anything.

CHEPURNOY. You've forgotten? Well, well. Did you know that, my friend? That whenever she hears some big word from you, she asks me what it means?

MELANIA (*offended*). Oh, you . . . Boris, you're a dreadful person. I have a very bad memory for foreign words, what's funny about that?

FIMA *enters, briskly sets the table by the window, and brings in the tea-things.*

PROTASOV. What was it you asked him?

MELANIA (*guiltily*). I forgot what hydatopyromorphism was.

CHEPURNOY. And I told her it was an aquatic firework.

PROTASOV (*laughs*). A what!?

LIZA *enters and busies herself at the table.*

MELANIA. You should be ashamed of yourself, Boris!

PROTASOV (*smiling*). You know, you two have a very odd relationship, you're like cat and dog the whole time. I'm sorry, maybe I'm speaking out of turn . . .

MELANIA. Oh, absolutely! Boris doesn't like me. We might as well be strangers. He was brought up in our aunt's house in Poltava, and I was raised at our uncle's in Yaroslavl. We're orphans, you see . . .

CHEPURNOY. Yes, from Kazan.

MELANIA. We didn't even meet until we were already grown up, and took an instant dislike to each other. Actually, Boris doesn't like anybody. He's had no success in life, and because of that he's at odds with everybody. He doesn't even visit me . . .

CHEPURNOY. You know, my friend, when her old husband was alive, I'd turn up at their house, and he'd ask me to treat him . . .

MELANIA. That's a lie.

CHEPURNOY. And I'd say to him: I can't be treating *all* the cattle . . .

LIZA. Boris Nikolaevich!

PROTASOV *gives an embarrassed laugh.*

CHEPURNOY. What, have I gone too far?

LIZA. Drink your tea.

CHEPURNOY. And get off home. I understand.

MELANIA. Pavel Fyodorych – you were going to show me some algies under the microscope, you remember?

PROTASOV. You mean algae. Yes, how can I . . . er . . . Yes, it's possible. I can show you right now, if you'd like.

MELANIA. Oh yes, please! I'd be delighted.

PROTASOV. Well, let's go. Only there's a bit of a stink in my room. (*Exits.*)

MELANIA. That's all right, I don't mind. (*Follows him out.*)

CHEPURNOY. What a performance! The cow fancies a spot of algae!

LIZA (*annoyed*). Boris Nikolaevich! You speak your mind, you're honest and straightforward, I know, but . . .

CHEPURNOY. Beat me right this instant!

LIZA. Why do you act so abominably? Why are you so hard, and unpleasant, why do you have to sneer all the time?

CHEPURNOY. I'm not acting, I'm not putting on a show.

LIZA. There's enough cruelty and nastiness in life as it is – so many terrible things. We should be gentler, we should be kinder.

CHEPURNOY. And why lie about it? People are cruel and nasty, it's their nature.

LIZA. No, that's not true!

CHEPURNOY. What do you mean, not true? That's what you yourself think, and that's how you feel. I mean, aren't you always saying people are animals, that they're coarse and dirty, and that you're afraid of them? Well, I know that too, and I believe you. But when you say we've got to love people, then I don't believe you. That's your fear speaking.

LIZA. No, you don't understand me!

CHEPURNOY. Maybe not. I can understand loving something useful or agreeable: to love a pig, because it gives us bacon or lard, or to love music, or a fine crayfish, or a picture. Human beings, however, are both useless and disagreeable.

LIZA. Good God! How can you say things like that?

CHEPURNOY. You have to speak the truth, as you feel it. Oh, I've had a stab at kindness. I picked a boy off the street once, thought I'd bring him up, give him an education. He stole my watch and cleared off. So then I took in a young girl, again off the street, you know what I mean – she was still very young . . . and I thought, well, we'll see how we get along, and we'll maybe even get married. Then one day she came home blind drunk, and spat right in my . . .

LIZA. Stop it! That's enough! You mustn't talk about these things, don't you understand?

CHEPURNOY. Why on earth not? It'll all have to come out one day, the whole of my life. Maybe I'd feel a bit cleaner if it did.

LIZA. You ought to get married.

CHEPURNOY. Ah! Now, that's what I say.

LIZA. Find yourself a nice girl.

CHEPURNOY (*calmly*). And you know perfectly well – I've found a nice girl. I've spent the past two years hanging round her, like a bear at a honey-pot.

LIZA. Oh, not that again, please. Dear Boris Nikolaevich, please don't! I've given you my last word – it's not going to change, not ever, that's absolutely final.

CHEPURNOY. Well, perhaps not. But us Ukrainians are stubborn, you know. Not even a maybe?

LIZA (*almost frightened*). No!

CHEPURNOY. All right, let's change the subject for the moment.

LIZA. You frighten me with that stubbornness of yours.

CHEPURNOY. Well, don't be afraid. Don't be afraid of anything.

A pause. ROMAN *is pottering about on the terrace.* LIZA *starts and looks out of the window.*

LIZA. Why do you treat your sister so badly?

CHEPURNOY (*coolly*). She's a fool. Besides which she's mean.

LIZA. God Almighty!

CHEPURNOY. All right, all right, I won't! God help the man who hasn't got a smooth tongue in his head! My sister, you say? Well, what is she? At the age of twenty she married a rich old man, why was that, do you think? So then she very nearly did away with herself, out of boredom and disgust with him: one time they had to cut her down from a stovepipe, she'd tried to hang herself; another time she swallowed ammonia. Eventually he died, and now she's running around mad after . . .

LIZA. And maybe you're to blame – why didn't you give her some support?

CHEPURNOY. Maybe it is my fault, but maybe I did try to support her.

LIZA. And to punish her for that.

CHEPURNOY. It's not just that. Look, you may not know why she comes here, but I do.

LIZA. No, no! I don't want to hear it, you're just guessing. You'd do better to ask yourself who gave you the right to judge her.

CHEPURNOY. And who gave *you* the right to judge, eh? People don't need anybody's permission to exercise that right. Asking people not to judge is like asking them not to eat.

MELANIA (*enters in a state of excitement, followed by* PROTASOV). Yes, yes, Pavel Fyodorych, I understand, but is that honestly the truth?

PROTASOV. Yes, of course it is. Everything's alive, life is everywhere. And there are mysteries everywhere. To move among the world of wonders, the profound enigmas of existence, to spend all one's mental energies on their solution – that's a genuinely human life, that's an inexhaustible well of happiness and life-giving joy! It's only in the sphere of the intellect that man can be truly free, only then is he *man*, when he's using his reason, only then is he pure and good! Good is a creation of the intellect. And without consciousness, there is no good! (*Hurriedly whips out his watch and looks at it.*) Anyway, you'll have to excuse me, I must go. Yes, I'm afraid I've got to, damn it! (*Exits.*)

MELANIA. Oh, if only you'd heard what he was saying in there . . . the things he was saying! To me alone, yes, to me, Melania! That's the first time in my life anyone's spoken to me like that . . . such marvellous things . . . and to me! Boris is laughing . . . what is it, Boris? (*A catch in her voice.*) All right, I'm not saying I understood all his ideas, I didn't say that, did I? I'm a fool. Liza, I'm funny, aren't I? Oh, my dear Liza, just imagine it: you go on through life, and it's as if you were asleep . . . and then suddenly you're jolted awake, you open your eyes, it's morning, the sun's shining, and right away you can see nothing but light! And you can breathe with your whole heart, you breathe such pure joy. It's like matins, on Easter morning . . .

CHEPURNOY. What are you on about?

LIZA. Have a drink of tea. Sit down. You're terribly excited.

MELANIA. You wouldn't understand, Boris. No, thanks, I won't have tea, I'm just going. You must forgive me, Liza, I've upset you. I'll go now – goodbye. Tell him I've gone away, please – tell him I'm very grateful, tell him he's all my joy. Oh, he's so clever, such a wonderful . . . (*Exits to the terrace.*)

CHEPURNOY. What *is* she on about? I don't understand.

LIZA. I do. Pavel had the same effect on me once. It'll be as if the scales were to fall from your eyes, and your mind, he says. Everything'll be so clear, and so harmonious, the mysterious and the simple, the vast and the insignificant. And then I discovered real life, full of filth and bestiality, mindless cruelty. My heart was gripped with fear and doubt, and that's when I ended up in hospital.

CHEPURNOY. You shouldn't think about it. Why keep on about the hospital? That was then, it's not now.

LIZA. It will be.

YELENA *and* VAGHIN *appear on the terrace.*

CHEPURNOY. Somebody's coming. Ah! It's Yelena Nikolaevna, and the artist. It's time I was leaving.

YELENA. Ah, Boris Nikolaevich! Is Pavel in his room, Liza? Pour me some tea, please. (*She exits to find her husband.*)

CHEPURNOY. You're looking a bit pale and dishevelled, Dmitri – why's that, I wonder?

VAGHIN. Really? I don't know. How's your painting coming along, Liza?

LIZA. I haven't been painting today.

VAGHIN. That's a shame. Paint has a calming effect on the nerves.

CHEPURNOY. You wouldn't think so, looking at you.

VAGHIN. Well, not every colour, of course.

LIZA (*starts*). No . . . not red.

CHEPURNOY. Anyway, I'm off – goodbye. I'm going down to the stream to catch crayfish. Later, I'll boil them up and eat them, drink some beer, and have a smoke. No, don't bother seeing me out, Liza, I'll come back again . . . tomorrow.

YELENA *enters*.

Goodbye, Yelena Nikolaevna!

YELENA. You're leaving? Goodbye.

VAGHIN. Is he busy?

YELENA. Yes. He'll be down soon.

VAGHIN. He's completely wrapped up in that idiotic scheme of his to create a homunculus.

YELENA. That's a terrible way to speak. You should be ashamed.

VAGHIN. Well, these damned pedants irritate me, with their fantastical rubbish! And I can't forgive him for his treatment of you. That's monstrous.

YELENA. I'm beginning to regret having allowed myself to be so frank with you.

VAGHIN. You've got to be a free person, and anyone who doesn't appreciate that deserves no mercy.

YELENA. And that's what they'll get, you wait and see.

VAGHIN. When? What are you waiting for?

YELENA. I've got to know how I stand . . . what place I hold in his heart.

VAGHIN. None whatsoever!

YELENA (*with a knowing smile*). Well, if that's the case, fine. Everything can be quite easily resolved: he doesn't need me, so I'll leave. But what if that's not so? What if he's simply used up all his love, if it's been somehow drawn down into the depths of his heart by the force of this obsession, this grand design of his. And I leave him, and suddenly his love flares up again . . .

VAGHIN. Is that what you want? Honestly?

YELENA. You know there'll be a fearful drama? And I hate scenes.

VAGHIN. It's him you're afraid for, isn't it.

YELENA. I don't want to disrupt his life.

VAGHIN. You're thinking it over – that means you don't want to do it. People who want something badly don't have to think.

YELENA. Beasts don't. Animals don't have to think. But a human being ought to act so that there's less evil in the world.

VAGHIN. Yes, to offer yourself up as a sacrifice, and so forth. Liza's having a bad influence on you with that morbid philosophy of hers.

YELENA. Evil is disgusting. And suffering is repellent. I think of suffering as a disgrace to oneself, and causing suffering to others is mean and shabby.

VAGHIN. Well, well, the voice of reason! Nevertheless, there's the spirit of a handmaiden speaking through you. You're offering yourself up as a sacrifice – to whom? A man who breaks life down into tiny particles, in a stupid effort to discover its origin? What an absurd idea! It's dark death he serves, not freedom, not beauty or joy. And he doesn't need your sacrifice.

YELENA. Please, Dmitri, calm down! I'm not talking about sacrifice. And I have no reason to trust the strength of your feelings.

VAGHIN. You don't trust in my love?

YELENA. Let's say, I don't trust myself.

LIZA enters.

VAGHIN. How cold you are.

YELENA. I'm being sincere with you.

LIZA. Pavel's been getting interrupted all day.

YELENA. By whom?

LIZA. Oh, everybody – Nanny, that blacksmith, the watchman.

YELENA. And was Pavel upset?

LIZA. I think so.

YELENA. That's annoying.

VAGHIN *goes out onto the terrace.*

LIZA. Yelena, I'm sorry, but it's terrible – you're paying so little attention to him.

YELENA. He's never said anything about it to me.

LIZA (*stands up*). Maybe that's because he doesn't like speaking to you. (*Goes upstairs to her room.*)

YELENA (*mildly*). Liza! Why must you . . . Liza, you're wrong. Listen to me, please.

LIZA *does not answer.* YELENA *watches her leave, shrugs, and then crosses slowly, frowning, to the terrace door.* FIMA *enters from the dining-room.*

FIMA. Ma'am!

YELENA. Yes? What is it?

FIMA. Melania Nikolaevna arrived while you were away, and she told me . . .

A pause.

YELENA (*abstractedly*). Yes? She told you what?

FIMA. It wasn't very nice.

YELENA. If it wasn't very nice, then don't say it.

FIMA. She told me . . . she said, keep an eye on the mistress – on you, that is.

YELENA. What do you mean? Honestly, Fima, you're forever inventing some stupid nonsense or other. Go away, please!

FIMA. It's not nonsense, my word of honour! She told me to keep an eye on the mistress and Mister Vaghin.

YELENA (*quietly*). Get out of my sight!

FIMA. It's not my fault! And look, she gave me a rouble.

YELENA. Get out!

FIMA *quickly exits.* PROTASOV *emerges hurriedly from behind the portière.*

PROTASOV. Lena, what are you shouting about, eh? Aha! At war with Fima, I see. You know, she's an amazing girl. She's got some special kind of skirts: they catch onto everything, knock everything over, bang into . . . I'd like a minute with you. Well, ten to be precise. Pour me some tea, please. So, Dmitri hasn't come?

YELENA. He's on the terrace.

PROTASOV. And is Liza there?

YELENA. She's in her room.

PROTASOV. You're a bit out of sorts, eh?

YELENA. I'm a little tired.

PROTASOV. So, how is your portrait coming along?

YELENA. You ask me that every day.

PROTASOV. Really? Ah, here's Dmitri, and looking angry. Why's that?

VAGHIN (*entering from the terrace*). Yes, I am. Anyway, one of these days I'm going to paint that garden of yours, just at this time of day, at sunset.

PROTASOV. And that's making you angry in anticipation?

VAGHIN. Are you trying to be funny?

YELENA. Will you have some tea?

PROTASOV (*rises*). Oh dear, you're both out of sorts. Well, I'm going into the kitchen. I've got my things in there. Pour me another glass, Lena. (*Exits.*)

VAGHIN. You know, one of these days he'll stick you into a retort, splash some sort of acid over you, and watch to see how you're enjoying it.

YELENA. Oh, don't talk rubbish. If you don't want to . . .

VAGHIN (*simply, sincerely*). Yelena, I've never experienced anything as powerful as the way I feel towards you. It torments me, but at the same time I feel elated.

YELENA. Really?

VAGHIN. I want to be exalted in your eyes, to be the best and brightest.

YELENA. That's good. I'm delighted for you.

VAGHIN. Yelena! Please believe me.

PROTASOV (*from the dining-room, then enters holding a metal dish*). Nanny, leave me alone, please! And why a cook, plus her husband? Just take the cook, if that's all we want, and leave me in peace!

YELENA. Nanny, I specifically asked you . . .

PROTASOV. I can't get rid of her – she sticks to me like glue, honestly! (*Exits to his room.*)

YELENA. Nanny, I asked you not to bother Pavel.

ANTONOVNA. Well, I'm sorry, Yelena Nikolaevna, but I'd just like to know who's master in this house. Pavel's too busy, Liza's a sick person, and you're not here for days on end.

YELENA. But you mustn't bother Pavel with trivialities.

ANTONOVNA. Well, you can look after it yourself, then.

YELENA. Huh! That's the last straw, you trying to teach me my . . .

ANTONOVNA. And why shouldn't I? When I see this house going to the dogs, and poor Pasha being ignored.

YELENA (*quietly*). Nanny, I'm asking you, please go away!

ANTONOVNA. Very well, ma'am. But not even the General's lady chased me out of this house. (*Exits, deeply offended.*)

YELENA *rises, paces agitatedly up and down the room.* VAGHIN *watches her with a mocking smile.*

YELENA. You find this amusing?

VAGHIN. Well, a little drop of stupidity's always amusing. (*Intensely.*) Yelena, you've got to get out of this house! You were created for a beautiful, free life . . .

YELENA (*abstractedly*). Is such a life possible, when we're surrounded by savages? You know, it's strange: the greater the man, the more pettiness there is about him . . . just the way the wind blows all kinds of trash up against a tall building.

PROTASOV *enters, pale and dejected-looking. There is something childishly helpless and touching about him, in his sincerity. He speaks quietly, and as if apologetically.*

What is it, Pavel? What's the matter?

PROTASOV. It's . . . it's deoxydized . . . d'you know what means? Yes, it's deoxydized. And the experiment was set up so rigorously. I was keeping a close watch on everything . . .

He looks at his wife, and it's as if he doesn't see her. He goes up to the table, sits down, and begins nervously tapping his fingers. He takes a notebook out of his pocket, writes something into it with a pencil, wholly absorbed in his task. VAGHIN *silently squeezes* YELENA's *hand and exits.*

YELENA (*quietly*). Pavel . . . (*A little louder.*) Pavel, dear, are you very upset? Really?

PROTASOV (*through clenched teeth*). Wait a minute . . . Why did it deoxydize?

Curtain.

Act Two

*To the right, the wall of the house and a wide terrace with a balustrade;
several of the balusters have fallen out. There are two tables on the terrace –
a large dining-table, and a small table in the corner, on which are scattered
dice and lotto counters. The rear side of the terrace is covered with an
awning. Along the whole length of the courtyard, as far as the fence at the
back, stands an old green-painted trellis, with the garden beyond. It is
evening.* CHEPURNOY *and* NAZAR AVDEYEVICH *emerge round
the corner of the terrace.*

NAZAR. So – it's nothing to worry about?

CHEPURNOY. Not really.

NAZAR. Good, good. I mean, she's no great shakes as a horse,
but she's still worth money. Sixty roubles she cost seven years
ago, and she's eaten God knows how much in oats since.
Anyway, if she isn't going to get better, you let me know, and
I'll sell her on.

CHEPURNOY. What, d'you think she'll recover with another
owner?

NAZAR. Well, it won't be my business then, will it. (*A pause.*) By
the way, Doctor sir . . .

CHEPURNOY. Yes, what is it?

NAZAR. Er . . . I've a slightly delicate request to make of you,
sir – the thing is, I don't know quite how to put it.

CHEPURNOY (*lighting a cigarette*). Put it briefly, sir.

NAZAR. Yes, yes, that's absolutely sensible. You see, if you'll
permit me to explain, my trifling little request . . .

CHEPURNOY. Briefer still.

NAZAR. Well, you see, it concerns Mr Protasov.

CHEPURNOY. Aha . . . go on.

NAZAR. Well, it's like this, sir – my son's learned all about manufacturing, in the commercial college, and he says chemistry's the coming thing. I mean, I can see it for myself – toilet soap, perfume, rouge – all those sort of goods go like hot cakes these days, and make big profits.

CHEPURNOY. In a nutshell, please.

MISHA *looks out from around the corner.* CHEPURNOY *notices him.*

NAZAR. No way I can, sir – this is a complicated enterprise. I mean, vinegar, for example, all kinds of essences, and a lot of other things. And here's me looking at Mr Protasov: he's wasting materials and time to no purpose, and they'll soon have nothing to live on, that's my opinion. Anyway, sir – have a word with him, do.

CHEPURNOY. A word about what – vinegar?

NAZAR. Well, generally speaking, yes. If you make the point, that they'll soon be left with no income. And I mean, I'll offer him a good deal: I'll set up a little factory for him and he can work on something profitable. He hasn't got the capital to be a partner, but I'd take a note of hand.

CHEPURNOY (*mocking*) Out of the kindness of your heart, eh?

NAZAR. I'm a kindhearted man! I mean, I see a person employed to no purpose, and right away I want to put that person to use in business. And he's one worth watching, yes, a gentleman of distinction. Heavens above, he put on a firework display for his good lady's birthday! Poetry in motion it was, a work of art. So, you'll have a word with him, yes?

FIMA *is preparing tea on the terrace.*

CHEPURNOY. I'll have a word.

NAZAR. You'll be doing him a real service, that's the long and the short of it. Anyway, in the meantime – goodbye.

CHEPURNOY. Goodbye. (*To* FIMA.) Where's your master and mistress?

FIMA. The master's in his room, and the mistress is in the garden, with Mr Vaghin. The young mistress is there.

CHEPURNOY. Right then, I'll go into the garden too.

MISHA (*emerging hurriedly from around the corner*). Excuse me, sir . . . I haven't had the pleasure of your acquaintance. I don't know your name.

CHEPURNOY. That's fine. I don't know yours either.

MISHA. Mikhail Nazarovich – at your service, sir!

CHEPURNOY. What service? I don't need anything from you.

MISHA (*condescendingly*). It's a manner of speaking, sir, a form of politeness. Anyway, I was an accidental witness to your conversation with my father.

CHEPURNOY. Yes, I saw that accident. Tell me, why do your feet keep twitching?

MISHA. That? Oh, that's from impatience, sir – to be up and doing. I have a very lively character.

CHEPURNOY. Up and doing what?

MISHA. I don't know what you mean, sir – it's just general high spirits.

CHEPURNOY. Ah, I see . . . well, goodbye.

MISHA. Please, sir – I have something to say to you.

CHEPURNOY. About what?

MISHA. It's on the matter of my father's suggestion. You see, it's actually my idea, only father didn't explain it to you very clearly.

CHEPURNOY. No, that's all right, I understood.

MISHA. Yes, sir, but perhaps you would do me the honour of coming to the Paris Restaurant, on Trinity Street, at nine o' clock this evening?

CHEPURNOY. No, sir, I won't do that honour even to you.

MISHA. Well, I'm sorry to hear that.

CHEPURNOY (*with a sigh of relief*). And so am I. (*Exits to the garden.*)

MISHA (*watches him go, contemptuously*). Ignorant pig. Huh, a genuine horse-doctor, that one.

FIMA. What? And you wonder why they won't talk to you?

MISHA. Yes, well, you know what I can do with you, Fima my love.

FIMA. Yes – nothing.

MISHA. I can say you stole that ring I gave you – the assistant police chief's a friend of mine.

FIMA. You don't scare me. He's chasing after me too, that police crony of yours.

MISHA. So much the worse for you. No, Fima, I was only joking. We need to have a serious talk. Twenty-five roubles, and the flat – is it a deal?

FIMA. Go to hell! I'm an honest woman.

MISHA. You're a fool, that's what you are. Wait, listen! There's another friend – Zotikov, he's quite good-looking, and rich. I'll introduce you to him if you like.

FIMA. You're too late! He's already sent me two letters – so there!

MISHA (*amazed and indignant*). What? You're making it up, surely. What a swine! Honestly – some people! Damn crooks, the lot of them. Not you, Fima – you're terrific . . . I mean, I'd marry you myself, if I didn't have to find a rich wife.

FIMA (*sotto voce*). Someone's coming.

LIZA *and* CHEPURNOY *emerge from the garden.*

LIZA (*to* MISHA). Yes? Is there something you want?

MISHA. No, no – I was just intimating to your maid that she shouldn't splash liquid chemicals out of the window into the garden. The vegetation suffers, and besides, these are dangerous times – there's cholera on the way, perhaps you've heard?

CHEPURNOY. Thank you, young man, and goodbye!

MISHA. Your servant, sir. (*Hurriedly exits.*)

LIZA (*walks out onto the terrace*). Really, what a brazen-faced creature.

CHEPURNOY. And my colleague here's trying to create living matter – what's the point? A pernicious creature like that? Or myself – also living matter, and what's the point of me?

LIZA. You're in such a bad mood today. Let's finish our game of lotto . . . sit down. I'll carry on: six, twenty-three . . .

CHEPURNOY. Ten, I've got twenty-nine . . .

LIZA. I don't understand you . . . Eight, thirty-one . . . I mean, you're so healthy, and strong . . .

CHEPURNOY. Seven, thirty-six . . .

LIZA. And yet you're not interested in anything, you don't do anything. Five, thirty-six . . . Nowadays, when life is taking on such a tragic colouring. Such hatred springing up everywhere, and so little love . . .

CHEPURNOY. Thirty-six? Ten, forty-one . . .

LIZA. And you could bring so much to this life with your work, good, clever work . . . I've got eight, forty-four . . .

CHEPURNOY. I'm already forty years old . . . and seven points . . . Forty-eight . . .

LIZA. Forty? That's nothing at all! Ten, fifty-four . . .

CHEPURNOY. And you've completely ruined me . . . Three, fifty-one . . .

LIZA. Me? I've ruined you?

CHEPURNOY. Yes. All of you. Your brother, Yelena Nikolaevna, yourself.

LIZA. Eight . . . I've won . . . Let's start again, only we'll not count aloud, it inhibits conversation. So, explain to me, in what way have we ruined you?

CHEPURNOY. Well, you know, up until we met, I had an intense curiosity.

LIZA. You were interested in things.

CHEPURNOY. Well, yes – curious . . . I wanted to know about everything. I'd see a new book, I'd read it, I'd want to know what was new about it apart from the cover. Some man'd be getting beaten up in the street – I'd stop and take a look, to see if they were beating him in earnest, and sometimes I'd even ask what they were beating him for. And I studied to be a vet with intense curiosity . . .

ANTONOVNA (*in the doorway*). Liza dear, have you taken your drops?

LIZA. Yes, yes.

ANTONOVNA. The samovar's boiling, and there's nobody at the table. Oh, Lord! (*Exits to the garden.*)

CHEPURNOY. Anyway, I looked on everything with a curious eye, and I saw that life was pretty much of a mess, that people were greedy and stupid, and that I was better, and cleverer than they. That was good to know, and my soul was at peace. Of course I could see that for some men, life was harder than for that horse I was treating, and worse even than a dog's. However, that circumstance could be explained by the fact that man is stupider than a horse or a dog.

LIZA. Why do you say things like that? Surely you don't believe it?

CHEPURNOY. As I said, that's how I lived, and it wasn't too bad a life. Then I happened to fetch up here, and I see that one person's totally wrapped up in science, another raves on about cinnabar and ochre; a third pretends to be bright and intelligent . . . and you've peered into things too deeply, and bear your tragic spirit everywhere.

LIZA. But in what way have we ruined you? I've won again . . .

CHEPURNOY. I don't know how to put it. At first I enjoyed being with you so much that I gave up drinking vodka, I found your conversations intoxicating enough. Then I lost my curiosity, and my peace of mind too.

ANTONOVNA (emerges from the garden). Would you like some tea now?

PROTASOV (from indoors). Is the samovar ready? Wonderful! My dear colleague, good morning!

CHEPURNOY. Good morning.

PROTASOV. So, is Lena in the garden?

LIZA. Yes . . .

PROTASOV. I'll go and call her. Hm . . . you're going to lose.

CHEPURNOY. I already have.

PROTASOV. You're a splendid colour today, Liza, and your eyes are so clear and calm. It's lovely to see. (*Exits to the garden.*)

LIZA (*annoyed*). Why does he always speak to me as if I was a sick child?

CHEPURNOY. That's how he is with everybody, if they've no interest in protoplasm.

LIZA. They all do that with me. They all keep reminding me that I'm unwell.

CHEPURNOY. You should forget about it yourself first.

LIZA. Anyway, please go on . . . you said you were getting worried – why?

CHEPURNOY. Worried, yes – and somehow uneasy. As if the mechanism of my soul had suddenly begun to rust. Liza, I'm finding this absurd, and if you won't help . . .

LIZA. Dear Boris Nikolaevich, please, let's drop the subject. I'm a cripple, ugly . . .

CHEPURNOY (*calmly*). Then I'll simply perish, like a dung-beetle.

LIZA (*leaps to her feet*). Please, no more! You're torturing me, don't you understand that?

CHEPURNOY (*alarmed*). All right, all right! I'm sorry. I'll say no more – please, calm down.

LIZA. Dear God, how terribly pathetic they all are. They're like all helpless people, so alone . . .

CHEPURNOY. You know, I used to sleep easy. Now, I lie awake, my eyes wide open, dreaming, like a lovesick student, not even out of first year. I want to do something – something heroic, you know? But what? I can't even begin to guess. It all seems to me like ice floating past on a river, and there's a little piglet sitting on an ice-floe, a tiny, reddish-coloured little piglet, and it keeps on whimpering. And suddenly I rush towards it, plunge into the water, and rescue the piglet! But alas, nobody wants it. And the really annoying thing is that I've got to eat that salvaged piglet all by myself, with sour cream . . .

LIZA (*laughs*). That's so funny.

CHEPURNOY. Yes, it'd make you weep.

YELENA, PROTASOV *and* VAGHIN *enter from the garden.*

LIZA. Shall I pour the tea?

CHEPURNOY. Go ahead, what else is there to do? You know, Liza, you ought to marry me just the same – we could go around moaning about the world together.

LIZA (*taken aback*). Really, the way you joke. It's so grim, and strange.

CHEPURNOY (*calmly*). Think about it, what else is there for you and me?

LIZA (*frightened*). Be quiet, please. That's enough.

YELENA. Well, yes, it's beautiful, but in terms of the idea, it's not very profound, and the subject wouldn't appeal to everybody.

VAGHIN. Art has always been the preserve of the few. That's its pride.

YELENA. That's its tragedy.

VAGHIN. Yes, that's the view of the majority, and for that reason alone, I'm against it.

YELENA. Oh, that's just a pose. Art should ennoble people.

VAGHIN. Art has no purpose.

PROTASOV. My dear friend, everything has a purpose in this world.

CHEPURNOY. That's if you don't count the world itself.

LIZA. Dear God! I've heard all this a thousand times!

YELENA. Dmitri Sergeyich – life is hard, people sometimes get tired of living. Life is harsh, isn't it? So how are we to restore our spirits? Beauty is extremely rare, but when something is truly beautiful, it warms my heart, like the sun suddenly lighting up a cloudy day. What's needed is for all people to understand and love beauty, and then they'll build their morality on it. They'll come to appreciate their own actions, as beautiful or ugly, and then life really will be wonderful!

PROTASOV. That's marvellous, Lena! And it is possible.

VAGHIN. What business have I got with people? I want to sing my own song, by myself, and for myself alone!

YELENA. Oh, stuff! What do we need all these words for? What's needed is for art to reflect the eternal longing of man, for the distant heights. And when that same longing exists in an artist, and when he believes in the radiant power of beauty, like the sun, then his painting, his book, his sonata – will become clear to me . . . precious. He'll call forth an answering chord in my soul, and if I'm tired, I'll be restored and want to work again, to feel happy and alive!

PROTASOV. Bravo, Lena, wonderful!

YELENA. You know, sometimes I dream about a painting: there's a boundless sea, and in the midst of it, there's a ship, caught up in the greedy embrace of the raging green waves, and at the prow of the ship stand these strong, powerful-looking people. They're just people, standing there on the deck, and they have such cheerful, open faces – smiling with pride, gazing into the distance, ready to die peacefully, if need be, on the way to their goal. And that's all there is in the picture.

VAGHIN. That's interesting. Yes.

PROTASOV. Wait . . .

YELENA. Now these same people would walk under the burning sun, across the yellow sands of the desert . . .

LIZA (*involuntarily, under her breath*). They're red.

YELENA. It doesn't matter. All that's needed is these special people, courageous and proud, unshakeable in their resolve – and simple, the way everything great is simple. A painting like that would make me feel proud of such people, and of the artist who had created them. And it would remind me of all those other great people who have helped to bring us so far away from the animals, and who are leading us still further towards humanity!

VAGHIN. Yes, I understand that. That's interesting . . . beautiful! Yes, I'll have a shot at that, dammit!

YAKOV TROSHIN *approaches the terrace, and unobserved, stands open-mouthed.*

PROTASOV. Of course you will, Dmitri. Paint it! Well done, Lena! That's . . . isn't that something new for you, Lena?

YELENA. How would you know if it's new or old?

TROSHIN. Er . . . my good sirs . . . your honours . . . (*They all turn towards him.*) I've been waiting till you finished your interesting conversation, but I'm afraid I have to disturb you. No problem.

CHEPURNOY. What do you want?

TROSHIN. Ah, I recognise a Ukrainian accent . . . no problem. That's because I've been in the Ukraine myself. I also play the flute.

CHEPURNOY. Yes, but what is it you want?

TROSHIN. Permit me, sir – everything's in order. Let me introduce myself – second lieutenant Yakov Troshin, former deputy stationmaster at Log . . . that same Yakov Troshin, whose wife and child were crushed to death by a train. I've still got childer, but no wife . . . no, sirs! With whom do I have the honour?

PROTASOV. You know, drunk people are so interesting.

LIZA (*reproachfully*). Pavel! How can you . . .

YELENA. What can we do for you?

TROSHIN (*bowing*). Forgive me, my lady. (*Shows her his foot, wearing a slipper.*) *Sans* bootee! Life's little ups and downs. My lady! Tell me, please, where Yegor the blacksmith lives. Yegor . . . I've forgotten his name. Maybe he hasn't even got a name. He might've come to me in a dream at night, eh?

YELENA. Round there, downstairs in the servants' wing.

TROSHIN. *Remerci, madame*! I've been looking for him all day. I'm so tired I can hardly stand. Round that corner? *Bon voyage*! He had the pleasure of making my acquaintance only yesterday, and here I am paying a visit. He'll appreciate this! Round the corner, you say? No problem! Till we meet again, *au revoir*!

PROTASOV. What a comical chap . . . *Sans* bootee, eh?

LIZA. Sssshh . . . Pavel . . .

TROSHIN (*makes to exit, swaying from side to side and muttering*). Aha! You think this is some nobody, eh? No, this is Yakov Troshin. He knows what's what, he knows how to behave . . . no problem! Yakov Troshin, yes! (*Exits.*)

PROTASOV. An amusing fellow, eh, Lena?

LIZA. So, what place will people like that occupy in your painting, Lena?

YELENA. They won't be in it, Liza.

PROTASOV. They're like seaweed, and barnacles, clinging to the bottom of the ship.

VAGHIN. And they'll impede its progress.

LIZA. So that's their fate, to perish, Yelena? Helpless and alone, these people will simply perish?

YELENA. They're already dead, Liza.

VAGHIN. And so are we – alone in the dark chaos of existence.

PROTASOV. Such people, my friend, are like the dead cells in any organism.

LIZA. Oh, you're all so heartless! I can't stand to listen to you – you're so blind, and cruel. (*Exits to the garden.* CHEPURNOY *slowly rises and follows her.*)

PROTASOV (*quietly*). You know, Lena, it's getting quite impossible to talk about anything when she's there. She turns everything around to the same thing, in that dark, sick corner of hers.

YELENA. I know. It's hard going with her. She lives in fear of life.

VAGHIN. Yelena Nikolaevna! Let's have somebody standing in the prow of the ship, and he'll have the face of a man who has buried all his hopes, left them behind on the shore. But his eyes will burn with the flame of a fierce resolve. And he sails on, to create new hopes – a man alone, even in the midst of solitude.

PROTASOV. And let's not have storms, please! Or rather, no – there can be a storm, but the ship's heading towards the sun, straight ahead. And you can call your painting 'To the Sun' – to the source of all life!

VAGHIN. Yes, the source of life! And there in the distance, amidst the storm clouds, like the sun, shines the face of a woman.

PROTASOV. Eh? Why a woman? I mean, presumably these people on the ship'll include Lavoisier and Darwin. Oh, anyway, I've talked too long, I must go . . . (*Quickly exits to his room.*)

VAGHIN (*sincerely*). As each day passes, my darling, I find myself ever more powerfully attracted to you. I'm ready to go down on my knees . . .

PROTASOV (*from his room*). Dmitri! A minute, please.

YELENA. Thou shalt not create unto thyself a false god, nor any likeness thereof.

VAGHIN. I'll paint that picture, you'll see! And it'll sing out, in its very colours, a magnificent hymn to freedom, to beauty.

PROTASOV. Dmitri!

YELENA. You'd better go, my friend.

VAGHIN *exits.* YELENA, *deep in thought, paces up and down the terrace.* CHEPURNOY's *voice can be heard from the garden.*

CHEPURNOY (*calmly*). But it can't be any other way. When a man speaks, he's human, but when he acts, he's still an animal.

LIZA (*sadly*). But when, tell me when . . .

They go out of earshot.

MELANIA (*walking in the courtyard*). Oh, Yelena Nikolaevna – you're at home.

YELENA (*drily*). Does that surprise you?

MELANIA. No, why should it? Hello.

YELENA. I'm sorry, but before I give you my hand . . .

MELANIA. Wha-a-at?

YELENA. I must ask you . . . Look, let's speak truthfully, straight out. You made an approach to my maid . . .

MELANIA (*hastily*). Oh, that little wretch – she's betrayed me.

YELENA (*after a pause*). So it's true? Melania Nikolaevna, you do understand what people . . . you know there's a name for that sort of behaviour?

MELANIA (*sincerely, heatedly*). Yes, yes, I know. It's all so simple, isn't it – oh, what's the difference? Listen to me, you're a woman, you're in love, maybe you can understand.

YELENA. Be quiet – your brother's in the garden.

MELANIA. Oh, who cares? Listen to me, Yelena – I love Pavel, and that's that! I love him so much, I'd willingly be his cook, or his maid. And you're in love, too, I can see it – I mean, you love that artist. You don't need Pavel. D'you want me to go down on my knees? Let me have him, please! I'll kiss your feet.

YELENA (*aghast*). What are you saying? What's the matter with you?

MELANIA. I don't care! I've got money, I can build him a laboratory. I'll build him a palace! I'll serve him, I won't let so much as a puff of wind touch him. I'll sit outside his door day and night, yes, I shall! Why should you have him, when I love him, worship him like a saint?

YELENA. Now just calm down, wait a minute. Obviously, I don't understand you.

MELANIA. My dear lady, listen to me! You're clever, you're well-bred, and pure. But I've had a hard life, frightful – I've seen nothing but second-rate people, worthless trash – and then he comes along! Yes, him! He's such a child . . . he's so exalted! Yes, and I'll be like an empress by his side. I'll be his servant, but to everyone else I'll be an empress! And my heart, my very soul will be able to breathe! I want a pure, good man! Do you understand me? There!

YELENA (*moved*). I find it difficult to understand you. We need to talk. Dear God, how unhappy you must be.

MELANIA. Yes! Oh yes! You can understand, you must. That's why I'm telling you this, because I know you'll understand, instantly. And you won't lie to me – maybe I can be human too, if you don't try to deceive me.

YELENA. I've no intention of deceiving you. I can feel the pain in your heart. Let's go to my room, come on.

MELANIA. What are you saying? Is it possible that you're a good person too?

YELENA (*takes her by the hand*). Believe me – please believe me, if people are sincere with one another, they'll understand.

MELANIA (*follows her out*). I don't know whether I believe you or not. Your words are clear, but your feelings . . . I can't understand. Are you a good person or not? You see, I'm afraid to believe in goodness. I haven't seen much of it. And as for myself, I'm a bad, dark-souled person. I've washed my soul in a sea of tears, but it's still dark . . .

They exit. ROMAN *looks round the corner with an axe in his hand.* LIZA *and* CHEPURNOY *enter from the garden, and* ANTONOVNA *from indoors.*

ANTONOVNA. Again – they've all gone running off in all directions, like half-wits. Liza, dear, why d'you keep wandering around? You ought to sit down.

LIZA. Nanny, leave me alone, please.

ANTONOVNA. There's no need to lose your temper. I don't know where you get the strength. (*Exits indoors, muttering.*)

CHEPURNOY. She's an old fusspot, but she does love you.

LIZA. No, she's just got into the habit of looking after us. She's been with the family more than thirty years. She's terribly stupid, and pigheaded. You know, it's strange – from as early as I can remember, we've always had music in the house, it's been lit up with the very finest ideas, dazzling, yet she hasn't become any kinder or cleverer for all that.

PROTASOV *and* VAGHIN *emerge from the interior.*

PROTASOV (*to* VAGHIN). You see, once the wood fibre has been chemically treated we'll be able to spin it, then you and I'll be wearing waistcoats made out of oak, jackets made out of birchwood . . .

VAGHIN. Oh, the hell with these wooden fantasies of yours — they're so boring.

PROTASOV. Well, really . . . it's you that's boring . . . Liza, pour me some tea!

CHEPURNOY. That's my sister's umbrella. My dear colleague! Melania asked me yesterday what relationship a hypothesis bore to a molecule. I told her a hypothesis was a molecule's grandmother!

PROTASOV (*laughing*). Why did you do that? She's so naive, and she is intensely interested in everything.

CHEPURNOY. Naive? Hm . . . But a monera and a monad are the foundlings of science, aren't they? I just mixed up the genealogy, that's all.

LIZA. You see what I mean? Even in your relationship with your sister, it's obvious how off-hand and spiteful people are with each other.

CHEPURNOY. Spiteful? What are you talking about?

LIZA (*agitated*). No, I'm telling you — there's more and more hatred piling up in this world, more brutality, increasing all the time.

PROTASOV. Liza! Is that you spreading your black wings again?

LIZA. Be quiet, Pavel! You see nothing, you're looking down a microscope.

CHEPURNOY. And what about you? A telescope? You shouldn't do that either — it's better to look with your own eyes.

LIZA (*disturbed, feverish*). Oh, you're all so blind! Open your eyes – everything you live by, your fine ideas, your feelings, they're like flowers growing in a forest, full of darkness and decay, full of horror. There's so few of you, you're scarcely noticeable in this world.

VAGHIN (*drily*). So tell us, who do you see in it?

LIZA. It's the millions I see in this world, not the hundreds, and hatred is growing among those millions. You're too intoxicated with your beautiful words and thoughts, you can't see that, but I've seen hatred erupting onto the streets, I've seen savage, malevolent people, shooting at each other, enjoying it. And one day, one day that hatred will burst in on you . . .

PROTASOV. Liza, this all so dreadful, obviously there's a thunderstorm on the way, it's so close, and your nerves can't . . .

LIZA (*pleading*). Please, don't talk to me about my illness!

PROTASOV. Well, honestly, who has any reason to hate me? Or him?

LIZA. Who? What about all those people you've left so far behind?

VAGHIN (*irascibly*). The hell with the lot of them! You can't go backwards for their sake.

LIZA. And you want to know why? Because you're alienated from them, you're utterly indifferent towards their harsh, inhuman lives! Because you're well fed and well dressed. Hatred is blind, yes, but you're bright and clear, it can see you all right!

VAGHIN. You make a good Cassandra.

PROTASOV (*excited*). Hold on, Dmitri! No, you're wrong, Liza. We're doing great and important work – he's enriching life with beauty, and I'm researching its mysteries. And those people you're talking about – in time they'll come to understand and appreciate our work.

VAGHIN. Whether they appreciate it or not, I couldn't care less!

PROTASOV. You shouldn't take such a gloomy view of them, Liza: they're better than you think — they're intelligent . . .

LIZA. Pavel, you know nothing.

PROTASOV. No, I do know, and I can see!

As he begins his speech, YELENA *and* MELANIA *emerge onto the terrace, both looking very agitated.*

I can see how life grows and develops, I can see it yielding to the relentless questing of my mind, opening up its profound and wonderful mysteries before me. I see myself already the master of many things, and I know that man will attain mastery over all things! Everything that grows becomes more complex — people are constantly raising their expectations, both of life, and of themselves. Under the sun's rays, some insignificant and shapeless lump of protein once flared up into life, multiplied itself, came together to form an eagle, a lion, a human being; and there'll come a time when out of us, mere people, out of all people, there will arise a magnificent, shapely organism — humanity! Yes, humanity, sirs! And then every cell will contain the past — the fulfilment of our great conquest of ideas — our work! The present will be free, comradely labour, carried out for the sheer pleasure of that labour, and the future — I can feel, I can see it — will be truly wonderful. Humanity is growing and maturing. That's life, that's what it means!

LIZA (*yearningly*). Oh, I wish I could believe that, I wish it so much.

She takes a notebook out of her pocket and writes something in it. MELANIA *is looking at* PAVEL *almost worshipfully, which seems rather comical.* YELENA's *expression, at the beginning severe, is now lit up with a melancholy smile.* VAGHIN *is listening animatedly,* CHEPURNOY *is bent low over the table, his face not visible.*

VAGHIN. I like you in your poetic vein.

PROTASOV. The fear of death – that's what stops us from becoming bold, beautiful, free people. It hangs over us like a dark cloud, covers the earth with shadows, out of which phantoms are born. It causes people to stray from the direct route to freedom, from the broad highway of experiment. It inspires them to construct hasty and ill-conceived speculations on the meaning of existence, it terrifies the reason, and then thought creates fallacies! But we, people like us, the children of the sun, of the bright source of life, we shall overcome the dark terror of death. We are the children of the sun, yes! That's what burns in our blood, that's what generates proud, fiery ideas, lighting up the gloom of our confusion – the sun, an ocean of energy and beauty, and intoxicating joy for the soul!

LIZA (*springing up*). Oh, Pavel, that's wonderful! The children of the sun . . . even me? Am I one? Quickly, Pavel, tell me! Am I?

PROTASOV. Yes, yes, you too – all people! Yes, of course!

LIZA. Truly? Oh, that's wonderful . . . I can't tell you . . . It's so wonderful! Children of the sun, yes? But my heart's broken, my heart's torn asunder – listen! (*She reads aloud, at first with her eyes closed.*)

'The eagle mounts up to the sky,
His strong bright wings outspread -
Oh, how I wish I could follow
There, where the eagle has led!
But all my efforts are in vain,
A daughter of this sad race,
For my soul's wings have long trailed
In the dust and dirt of this place . . .
Yes, I love your fierce quarrels,
The bright fire of your vision,
But I know of deep dark lairs,
And blind moles there imprisoned;
Beauty and truth are to them unknown;

They take no joy in the sun;
Desperate need is all they feel,
And want of love each one.

Like a stone wall of silence
Between us still they stand -
Tell me, what words can I speak
To raise them up from this land?'

They all look at her in silence a few moments. VAGHIN *is unhappy at her excitement.*

PROTASOV. Liza, is that yours? Do you really write poetry?

YELENA. That was well spoken, Liza. I understand you.

VAGHIN. Sirs, if you'll allow me? Liza, I know some other verses, which might serve as a reply to yours.

LIZA. Go ahead.

VAGHIN.
'Like sparks in a cloud of black smoke,
In the midst of life we are alone.
But we are the seeds of the future,
The lights of the time to come;
For we serve in Freedom's bright temple,
And Beauty and Truth seek to know,
So that these self-same blind moles
Might one day to eagles grow!'

PROTASOV. Bravo, Dmitri! Wonderful, my dear friend!

MELANIA (*in ecstasy*). Oh, Lord! How fine . . . Yelena Nikolaevna, I do understand her . . . I do . . . (*Begins to weep.*)

YELENA. Calm down. Please, don't . . .

LIZA (*sadly*). Yes, you can feel triumphant, but I feel nothing but pity. It makes me sad to see so many fine ideas, flaring up and then vanishing, like sparks in the darkness of night, without having lit up the road for people. That makes me sad.

MELANIA (*kissing* PROTASOV's *hand*). Oh, thank you, thank you, my bright angel!

PROTASOV (*embarrassed*). What are you doing? Why are you doing that? My hands might be dirty.

MELANIA. They can't be.

LIZA. Boris Nikolaevich, what's the matter with you?

CHEPURNOY. Nothing, I'm just listening.

LIZA. I spoke well, didn't I.

CHEPURNOY. From you came truth.

LIZA. From me, really?

MELANIA (*to* YELENA). I'm leaving now. Oh, my dearest friend! (*Goes indoors.*)

YELENA *follows her.*

CHEPURNOY. And from him came beauty.

VAGHIN. And which is better?

CHEPURNOY. Yes. Beauty is better, but people have more need of truth.

LIZA. And what about you? Which do you need?

CHEPURNOY. I don't really know. A bit of both, maybe – in moderation, of course.

YELENA (*re-enters*). Pavel, Melania Nikolaevna's calling for you.

PROTASOV. Lena, really, I mean, why did she kiss my hand? It's so silly and unpleasant!

YELENA (*mocking*). Yes, it's a hard life.

PROTASOV (*makes to exit*). And her lips are greasy. What on earth does she want? (*Goes indoors.*)

From around the corner of the terrace AVDOTIA *is heard hysterically shouting.*

AVDOTIA. That's what you think, you swine!

LIZA (*gasps*). What's going on! Who is it!

AVDOTIA (*runs out*). Hah! Missed, you devil!

YEGOR (*holding a birch log in his hands*). Stop! Just stay there, I'm telling you!

LIZA. Oh my God! Hide her, somebody!

AVDOTIA (*running out onto the terrace*). Oh sirs! Oh, please, help me! He's going to kill me!

YELENA. Come here! Quickly!

AVDOTIA (*to her husband*). Hah! How do you like that, eh? (*Exits with* YELENA *into the house.*)

CHEPURNOY. Huh, that drunken idiot again. (*To* LIZA.) I think you'd better go in.

LIZA. For God's sake . . . For God's sake, stop him!

TROSHIN (*enters from round the corner*). Watch out, Yegor!

CHEPURNOY (*to* YEGOR.) Get away from here!

VAGHIN. Throw him out!

PROTASOV *comes rushing out of the house, followed by* MELANIA.

PROTASOV. Yegor, it's you again!

YEGOR (*to* CHEPURNOY). You can go to hell! Give me my wife!

PROTASOV. Have you gone mad?

TROSHIN. A wife belongs to her husband, my dear sir! Simple as that!

YEGOR. You're not hiding her from me. I'll come and get her!

ROMAN *enters, sleepily. He stands behind* YEGOR.

ROMAN. Yegor, don't start a row!

CHEPURNOY. Just you try!

LIZA. Boris Nikolaevich, he's got a club!

CHEPURNOY. Don't worry! Liza, please go.

PROTASOV. Liza, go inside, please.

YEGOR. Give her back to me! What's it to do with you? It's none of your business!

MELANIA. Watchman, call the police!

ROMAN. Yegor, I'm going to call the police.

YEGOR. Sir! Now, hold on, I've got a visitor here . . .

TROSHIN. Yes, no problem!

YEGOR. He's an educated man, with the heart of a . . .

TROSHIN. Absolutely true!

YEGOR. And she slapped him in the clock with a wet dishrag!

TROSHIN. That's a fact! Only not the clock, Yegor, it was the face.

PROTASOV. My dear sir! Now look, be a man . . .

YEGOR. I want her out here!

VAGHIN. Damn the man! What an amazing face!

MELANIA. Watchman! I've told you, go and fetch the police! Keep him there, seize him!

ROMAN. Yegor! I'm going, I tell you.

YEGOR (goes onto the terrace). All right, if you don't understand what I'm saying . . .

LIZA. Run quickly! He's coming! He'll kill her!

CHEPURNOY (goes to confront YEGOR, grimly). Right then, you just try.

PROTASOV. Liza, go away, please! (Leads her forcibly indoors.)

MELANIA follows them.

YEGOR. Get away, you . . . (*Holding his club in readiness.*)

CHEPURNOY (*looking him straight in the eye*). Well, go on.

YEGOR. I'll brain you.

CHEPURNOY (*to* YEGOR, *quietly*). No you won't, you miserable cur.

YEGOR. Don't you snarl at me.

CHEPURNOY. Go on, hit me.

YEGOR. Huh, you hit me! Right then . . . (*Flings his stick aside.*)

CHEPURNOY. Clear off! D'you hear?

TROSHIN (*despairingly*). Come on, Yegor, you'd better back off . . .

YEGOR (*retreating*). Huh! You damned devil, you!

CHEPURNOY (*contemptuously*). A whipped cur.

TROSHIN (*to* VAGHIN). *Bon soir, monsieur!* I mean, the family circle mustn't be disrupted, right?

VAGHIN. Go away.

CHEPURNOY (*descends from the terrace, walks up to* YEGOR). And you're on your way too, right? (*To* YEGOR.) If it wasn't for the fact there are ladies present, I'd sort out the pair of you.

TROSHIN (*making his way out behind* YEGOR). Superior force rules, sir – simple as that. (*Disappears round the corner.*)

CHEPURNOY (*returning to the terrace*). What a brute.

VAGHIN. Well, you had some look on your face. I couldn't help admiring it – very expressive!

PROTASOV (*enters*). What, have you chased them away?

LIZA (*hurriedly entering, to* CHEPURNOY). He . . . he didn't hit you? He didn't touch you?

CHEPURNOY. Ah! No, it's not that easy.

YELENA *and* MELANIA *enter.*

PROTASOV. God knows what's going on. I'm not going to give him any more work. Look, my hands are still trembling. Look, Lena . . .

VAGHIN. He's quite capable of killing somebody.

CHEPURNOY (*mocking*). So what about these, my dear colleague – scum like that? Are they children of the sun too?

LIZA (*suddenly*). You were lying, Pavel! There's not going to be anything, life's full of beasts! Why do you keep going on about the joys of the future, why? Why do you deceive us all, yourself and other people? You've left real people so far behind you. You're lonely, and unhappy, and petty – don't you really understand the horror of this life? Dear God, you're surrounded by enemies, there are beasts everywhere! We've got to get rid of cruelty, we've got to overcome hatred! For God's sake, try to understand me! Do you hear!

She becomes hysterical.

Curtain.

Act Three

The setting is the same as for Act One. An overcast day. YELENA *is sitting in an armchair by the wall.* LIZA *is pacing agitatedly about the room.*

YELENA. You shouldn't get so worked up.

LIZA. I'm ill, all right, but my thoughts are healthy!

YELENA. Has anyone said they weren't?

LIZA. What I have to say is so banal and dreary, I know that – you're fed up listening to me. You don't want to hear the truth about life, the tragedy of it all.

YELENA. Liza, you're exaggerating.

LIZA. No, I'm not! Just look at the gulf that separates you from your cook.

YELENA. And you think that'll somehow vanish, if I stand on the edge and start weeping, trembling with fear?

LIZA. But how can you carry on so calmly, when there are people who don't understand you? I can't live like that. I'm afraid of people who don't understand me! That's what's making me ill. Yelena, there have to be sacrifices. Do you understand? We need to sacrifice ourselves.

YELENA. Yes. Yes, freely, joyfully, in a transport of delight! But not by doing violence to ourselves – no, Liza! That's unworthy.

ANTONOVNA (*entering from the dining-room*). Yelena Nikola-evna . . .

LIZA (*irritated*). Nanny, what do you want?

ANTONOVNA. Now now – it's not for you. The landlord's here.

LIZA. Oh, let him wait. Go on, Nanny. (ANTONOVNA *exits.*)
So, am I wrong?

YELENA. I didn't say that.

LIZA. Can't you see how lonely we all are?

YELENA. No, I don't feel that.

LIZA. You just don't want to talk to me. I get on everyone's
nerves. You all want to enjoy life, and turn a blind eye to
anything nasty or frightening.

YELENA. Liza, you can't make yourself feel something.

LIZA. And what about you? You have a rotten life, but you're
too proud to admit it, even to yourself. I mean, I can see how
things are between you and Pavel.

YELENA. Drop it, please.

LIZA. Aha – you see? It's painful, isn't it.

YELENA. No. No – it's distasteful, that's all.

LIZA. It's painful! And you should let it hurt. It would bring you
to life. Oh, Yelena, you're so alone! You're so unhappy.

YELENA. And you're overjoyed, aren't you. Liza, that isn't nice.
What is it you want?

LIZA. What do I want? (*A pause, then fearfully.*) I don't know. I
don't know what I want! I'd like to live, but I don't know how
to. I can't! I don't feel I've any right to live the way I'd like
to. I'd like to have a kindred spirit, a soul-mate. I need some
respite from all my fears, and there's no-one to give it to me!

YELENA (*takes her hand*). Forgive me, but surely Boris . . .

LIZA. What right have I? I'm sick, aren't I? That's what you all
tell me. Oh, you tell me that often enough! Too often! Let me
go. I can't talk about that. Please, go away. Leave me!

Hurriedly exits to her room. YELENA *sighs deeply, begins pacing back and forth, her hands clasped behind her head. She comes to a halt before her husband's portrait, looks at it a few moments, biting her lip. She lets her hands fall, dejected.*

YELENA (*in a half-whisper*). Goodbye.

ANTONOVNA *enters.*

ANTONOVNA. Is it all right for the landlord now?

YELENA. Yes. Yes, all right.

ANTONOVNA (*exiting*). You can go in now, Nazar Avdeyich.

NAZAR. The very best of health to you, dear lady!

YELENA (*nodding*). What can I do for you?

NAZAR (*smirking, a little embarrassed*). Well, the fact is . . . you see, I was really looking for Mr Protasov.

YELENA. He's busy.

NAZAR. Hm . . . I don't know as I can tell you.

YELENA. Go ahead – I'll pass it onto him.

NAZAR. Well, it's a bit awkward, you see.

YELENA. As you wish.

NAZAR. Well, it makes no difference. The police've come, you see, about the smell – about them cesspits, and the other places.

YELENA (*frowning*). What's that got to do with my husband?

NAZAR. Well, he's no worse than other folk, of course – we're all to blame. But the police, you see, because of the cholera, they're saying there shouldn't be any smells. They don't take into account things that's supposed to smell, well, they'll give off a smell no matter what – anyway, they're talking about fining people, up to three hundred roubles.

YELENA (*disgusted*). Look, what is it you want?

NAZAR. I'm looking for a bit of advice, ma'am – to see if it's possible to spray some sort of chemical around, against the smell.

YELENA (*indignantly*). Now you listen to me . . . (*Checks herself.*) Well, all right – I'll give him the message. Goodbye!

NAZAR. You'll tell him right away?

YELENA (*exiting*). Nanny'll give you his answer.

NAZAR (*calling after her*). I'm much obliged. Huh, stuck-up madam! Well, you just wait – I'll twist your tail all right!

He exits. PROTASOV *and* YELENA *emerge from behind the portière.*

PROTASOV. Oh, and Yelena, would you send for Yegor, please?

YELENA. What, Yegor again?

PROTASOV. Well, we can't do without him, can we. He's very handy, and so quick on the uptake – you should see the brazier he's made me, absolutely a work of art! Quite exquisite. Heavens, what a dull day. No sitting, then?

YELENA. No. Anyway, when can we have a talk?

PROTASOV. Oh, not till this evening, please. Yes, I'm free this evening! What, are you bored? So where's Dmitri?

YELENA. I presume he's got other things to do besides keeping me amused.

PROTASOV (*failing to understand*). Yes . . . Hm! Yes, no doubt. You know, this while back, I've been looking at you, and I think . . . oh, I don't know, there's something different about you. Something significant . . .

YELENA. Really?

PROTASOV. Yes, there is. Anyway – I must disappear, like a puff of smoke! (*Exits to his room.*)

FIMA (*entering*). Oh, ma'am, please – let me go!

YELENA. What, this afternoon? But who's going to serve tea?

FIMA. No, I mean let me go for good. Pay me off.

YELENA. Oh, all right. But fetch Yegor first, please.

FIMA (*firmly*). I'm not going to Yegor's, ma'am.

YELENA. Why not?

FIMA. I don't want to, ma'am.

YELENA. Then send Nanny to me.

FIMA. Nanny's gone for a walk, down to the graveyard.

YELENA. I'll let you go when she comes back. Send the watchman in – can you do that?

FIMA. Yes, ma'am. So, you'll pay me off today, won't you. (*Exits.*)

YELENA (*calling after her*). Yes, yes.

CHEPURNOY *appears in the veranda doorway.*

CHEPURNOY. Why don't you keep your doors shut? Good afternoon!

YELENA (*giving him her hand*). I don't know . . . the servants seem distracted today.

CHEPURNOY. They're afraid of the cholera.

YELENA. It's spreading, apparently.

CHEPURNOY. It'll pass. Is Liza at home?

YELENA. She's in her room.

CHEPURNOY. Is she feeling all right?

YELENA. So-so. She's not particularly well, same as usual.

CHEPURNOY (*anxiously*). Mm . . . She's a tragic soul.

YELENA. Boris Nikolaevich, forgive me, I don't want to interfere, it's none of my business, but – well, it's quite important . . .

CHEPURNOY. Oh? What is it?

YELENA. Liza told me you had proposed to her . . .

CHEPURNOY (*hastily*). How did she tell you?

YELENA. What do you mean, how?

CHEPURNOY. Well, what did she look like? Did she make a
face? Was she laughing about it?

YELENA (*surprised*). Good heavens, no! She was overjoyed.

CHEPURNOY. Really? Is that the truth?

YELENA. Yes, it is. There was a kind of quiet joy . . . it was so
nice.

ROMAN *appears at the veranda door.*

CHEPURNOY. I'm such a fool! An absolute ass!

ROMAN. Is that me you're calling?

CHEPURNOY. No no – nobody's calling you. I was shouting at
myself, silly.

YELENA. Actually, I sent for him. Tell the smith I want to see
him, Roman.

ROMAN. What, Yegor?

YELENA. Yes.

ROMAN. Right now?

YELENA. Yes, yes.

ROMAN. All right (*Exits.*)

CHEPURNOY (*joyfully*). Give me your hand, and let me . . .
there, I'll kiss it! You've given me a present – there! Things
come to us when we least expect them – joys as well as
sorrows.

YELENA. I'm sorry – I don't understand.

CHEPURNOY. Oh, for Heaven's sake – don't you see? She was overjoyed, you say, when she told you I'd asked her to marry me?

YELENA. She was, I assure you.

CHEPURNOY (*triumphantly*). And yet she turned me down!

YELENA (*smiling*). Forgive me – this sounds so funny . . .

CHEPURNOY. Of course it's funny! It's just as I thought, you see – she doesn't want to marry me, but it's not that she can't stand me, it's because she's afraid of her illness.

YELENA. Yes, you're right.

CHEPURNOY. Anyway, I know what to do now. I'll come at her like a snowball rolling downhill, yes! What a piece of luck! It's a wonderful thing, luck, you know.

YELENA. Well, you'd better take off that tie – she doesn't like red.

CHEPURNOY (*laughs*). I put it on deliberately, just to tease her. It doesn't matter now, whether it's red or green – it's all the same. I can't go to her without a tie. Thank you!

Makes to exit. YEGOR *appears at the dining-room door, bewildered and dishevelled-looking.*

Ah! An old acquaintance. Here, give me your hand – let's make peace, right? There you are, my bold warrior! (*exits.*)

YELENA (*to* YEGOR). I'll speak to you in a minute.

YEGOR (*dully*). Ma'am, wait . . .

YELENA. What is it?

YEGOR. It's the wife, ma'am. She's not well.

YELENA. What's the matter with her?

YEGOR. She keeps being sick.

YELENA (*alarmed*). Has she been like that long?

YEGOR. Since this morning. She's calling for you all the time, ma'am. Go and get the mistress, she says, or I'm done for.

YELENA. So why didn't you send for me? Honestly, you'd think . . .

YEGOR. I was too ashamed, ma'am. After kicking up a row here.

YELENA. Oh, don't be silly – I'll go and see her.

YEGOR. No, ma'am, wait – I'm afraid.

YELENA. Afraid of what?

YEGOR. Maybe it's cholera.

YELENA. Nonsense! There's nothing to be afraid of.

YEGOR (*asking, but almost a demand*). Yelena Nikolaevna, you've got to cure her!

YELENA. She needs a doctor. You go into town right now.

YEGOR. She don't need no doctor, I don't believe in them! You can do it.

PROTASOV (*entering*). Aha! So the bold warrior's here, is he?

YELENA (*hurriedly*). Pavel, wait! His wife's been taken ill.

PROTASOV. Well, you see, if you will beat her . . .

YELENA. He thinks it's cholera. I'm going over there now, and you can . . .

PROTASOV (*alarmed*). You're going there? No, Lena, please – why you?

YELENA (*surprised*). Why not me?

PROTASOV. But, Lena, if it is cholera . . .

YEGOR (*barely suppressing a snarl*). Let her die, is that what you mean? Is that it? Are we not people, then?

YELENA. Oh, stop it, Yegor. Pavel, you're so tactless.

PROTASOV. But what do you know about it, Lena? You're not a doctor. And cholera's no joke, it's extremely dangerous!

YEGOR (*angrily*). And the people that's dying of it, it's not dangerous for them?

PROTASOV (*to* YEGOR). Look, please don't shout at me!

YELENA (*reproachfully*). Pavel! Come on, Yegor, let's go.

PROTASOV. I'll come too. This is foolhardy, Lena.

All three, YEGOR *leading, exit to the dining-room, from where their voices can still be heard.*

YELENA. No, Pavel – go back and telephone for a carriage.

PROTASOV. It's a doctor she needs, not you. What can you do? (*Re-enters, visibly upset.*) What can she do, in a case like this? Nanny! Damn! Damn! She wouldn't let me go. Fima! Or Nanny! Is everybody dead? Fima! (FIMA *hurries in.*) I'm shouting my head off here, while you're admiring yourself in your mirror.

FIMA (*offended*). I was not – I was polishing the silver.

PROTASOV. Well, leave that! I want you to go to Yegor's.

FIMA (*resolutely*). No, sir, I'm not going there.

PROTASOV. Why not? Your mistress is there.

FIMA. I don't care, sir.

PROTASOV. But why not?

FIMA. It's the cholera, sir!

PROTASOV (*mimicking her*). Oh, it's the cholera, sir! And that's where the mistress has gone, sir!

The door-bell rings.

FIMA. That's the door-bell, sir.

PROTASOV. Yes, sir! Well, answer it, sir! (FIMA *hurries out.* PROTASOV *watches her go.*) Sir this, sir that! Hissing like a snake . . . Oh yes, the telephone, dammit! (MELANIA *enters.*) Oh, it's you. Have you heard the news? There's cholera in the village – that's charming, isn't it. And Yelena's gone off to cure it, no less. How d'you like that?

MELANIA. Oh dear, oh dear! So you've got it too? My neighbour, the Colonel – his cook was taken away yesterday. And Yelena's gone to nurse them? Why on earth did she do that?

PROTASOV. God knows! Truly, 'tis a great mystery.

MELANIA. Why did you let her go?

PROTASOV. Why? I don't know. Oh yes, the telephone . . . (*Hurries out to his own room.*)

FIMA (*entering from the dining-room*). Good morning, ma'am.

MELANIA (*disapprovingly*). Hm! Good morning, your beautyship!

FIMA. Ma'am, I have a big favour to ask you.

MELANIA. What is it?

FIMA. I'm getting married.

MELANIA. So?

FIMA. To a respectable gentleman, ma'am – very respectable!

MELANIA. Who is it?

FIMA. Your neighbour, ma'am.

MELANIA (*starts back in astonishment*). Not the Colonel, surely?

FIMA (*modestly*). Heavens, no, ma'am! No, it's Mr Kocherin.

MELANIA. What, him? That old devil? Ugh! Good God, he's nearly sixty – rheumatism and everything. Why have you decided to do that, Fima? Money, I suppose. Well, I feel sorry for you, girl. No, no, get rid of him – him and his money!

FIMA. I've made my mind up, ma'am. It's all arranged.

MELANIA. Is it? Pity. So, what do you want from me?

FIMA. Well, ma'am, I've been raised an orphan, you see, and I thought maybe you wouldn't mind standing in as godmother for me.

MELANIA (*makes a rude gesture at her, the 'fig'*). Huh! Bite on that! So, how much did you sell me to your mistress for, eh?

FIMA (*taken aback*). Me, ma'am?

MELANIA. Yes, you, ma'am! How much?

FIMA (*recovering her composure*). Well, I'm sorry, ma'am – I thought that seeing as how you'd once sold yourself to an old man, you'd . . .

MELANIA (*crushed*). What? What did you say?

FIMA. I thought you'd maybe help me to do the same.

MELANIA (*thickly*). How dare you!

FIMA (*cool and collected*). I mean, you know yourself it's better getting fixed up that way, than going on the streets. At least it's only with one of them, not a hundred.

MELANIA (*horrified, quietly*). Go away. Go on, get out of my sight. I'll . . . I'll give you some money – just go away! I'll give it to you!

FIMA. Thank you very much, ma'am. When?

MELANIA. Go away! I haven't any with me!

FIMA. I'll come and see you this evening. You won't let me down?

MELANIA. No! Now go away, for Christ's sake!

FIMA *makes a leisurely exit.* MELANIA *slumps heavily into an armchair and begins weeping, moaning as if in pain.* PROTASOV *enters from his room.*

PROTASOV. She isn't back yet, is she? What is it? What's the matter with you?

MELANIA (*falling to her knees*). Oh, blessed angel! Save me, your slave!

PROTASOV (*startled*). What did you say? Get up, please. What are you doing?

MELANIA (*clasping his legs*). I'm drowning in filth. I'm drowning in my own vileness. Give me your hand! There's no-one better than you on this earth!

PROTASOV (*alarmed*). Look, stop it, I'm going to fall! And . . . and don't kiss my trousers, please! What's the matter with you?

MELANIA. I've committed a crime, I've sullied my soul – I need you to cleanse it, please! Who else but you can do that?

PROTASOV (*trying to understand*). Look, sit down . . . no, stand up, I mean! Right, now sit down. What is it you want?

MELANIA. Take me to your heart! Let me live here with you, just to see you every day, to hear your voice. I'm rich – you can take all of it! You can build yourself a proper study, for your science. You can build a great tower! Climb to the top, and live there, and I'll stay down below, I'll stand by the door day and night, and not let anyone near you. You can sell all my houses, all my land, everything, take it all, Pavel!

PROTASOV (*smiling*). Really? Well, that's an idea. Dammit, it certainly is! Just think what a laboratory I could build!

MELANIA (*delightedly*). Yes, yes! And take me, please, so I can see you always. You don't need to speak to me – just look at me now and again, just smile at me! I mean, if you had a dog, you would smile at it. You'd pat it now and again, wouldn't you? That's how I'll be – I'll be your little dog!

PROTASOV (*worried*). Wait, hold on. Why are you going on like this? This is most peculiar – don't please! I'm utterly astonished – I'd no idea you'd get so carried away . . .

MELANIA (*not listening*). I'm stupid, I know, I'm an absolute dimwit! I don't understand any of your books – you didn't think I'd read them?

PROTASOV (*bewildered*). You haven't? Then what have you . . .

MELANIA. Oh, my darling! I've kissed your books. I look inside them, and there are such words in them, words that nobody but you could understand. And I kiss them . . .

PROTASOV (*embarrassed*). So that's why the covers are all stained. But why on earth do you kiss books? This is some sort of fetish, surely.

MELANIA. I love you, don't you understand? Just to be near you, it's so wonderful – so pure and clear! You're like a god to me, you're divine, I love you!

PROTASOV (*quietly, awestruck*). I'm sorry . . . I mean, in what way?

MELANIA. Like a dog! I can't speak, I can only keep silent – and I've kept silent these many years, while the skin's been flayed from my very soul!

PROTASOV (*beginning to hope he might be mistaken*). I'm sorry, you must forgive me. I'm not sure I grasp your basic idea. Perhaps you'd better . . . I mean, shouldn't you discuss this with Lena?

MELANIA. I've spoken with her. She's a wonderful woman, and she knows you don't love her.

PROTASOV. What d'you mean, don't love her? What are you talking about?

MELANIA. She knows everything, she feels everything. Oh, she's so good! But what's the point of having two fires in the same room? She's a proud woman . . .

PROTASOV (*again at a loss*). You know, all this . . . it's all such a mix-up! Actually, I've never felt so ridiculous.

MELANIA. And when I'm with you at last – when you're finally mine . . .

PROTASOV (*slightly irritated*). What? What d'you mean, mine? (*Looks at her a moment, then speaks quietly, almost fearfully.*) Melania Nikolaevna, let's get this straight. You must forgive me, if I put a blunt question to you. Are you by any chance in love with me?

MELANIA (*looks at him a few moments also, then speaks, lowering her voice*). That's what I'm trying to say. Oh, my darling! That's what I'm saying!

PROTASOV. Really? I'm sorry . . . I thought . . . I thought . . . I was sure you didn't . . .

MELANIA (*softly*). I know – that's why I went too far.

PROTASOV (*begins nervously pacing around the room*). Well, I'm flattered, of course. I'm deeply touched. But unfortunately . . . I mean, I'm a married man . . . no, it's not that! You see, this isn't something one can decide on the spot, no, indeed! But Lena doesn't need to know about this, you understand – we'll work something out together.

MELANIA. She already knows.

PROTASOV (*almost in despair*). What d'you mean, knows?

CHEPURNOY and LIZA *come downstairs. They pass silently through the room to the veranda. CHEPURNOY is gloomily calm, LIZA excited.*

MELANIA (*quietly*). Oh, someone's coming! Sshhh . . . oh, it's my brother!

PROTASOV (*to LIZA*). Ah . . . hm! You're . . . you're going out?

CHEPURNOY (*dully*). Yes.

A pause.

PROTASOV (*sincerely and simply*). Melania Nikolaevna! This is an extraordinary situation, I'm sure you'll agree. An impossible situation. No doubt you think I'm being funny, and you're offended. But, my dearest lady, this is all so strange, I don't need this!

MELANIA. Don't need?

PROTASOV. No, no, I'm sorry! And I'll have to tell all this to Lena. And after that . . . Look, I'll have to go, she's still down there, and I'm worried about her. I can't not tell her. Please don't be angry.

Exits to his own room. MELANIA *quietly follows him out, then returns, bewildered and pathetic.*

MELANIA (*to herself*). I didn't get through to him. I'm so ashamed. (YELENA *enters from the veranda.*) Oh, my dear – have pity on a complete fool!

YELENA. What is it? Did you . . . did you tell Pavel?

MELANIA. I told him everything.

YELENA. And what did he say?

MELANIA. All my words . . . all my love . . . like water off a duck's back.

YELENA (*simply and sincerely*). I feel for you. What did he say?

MELANIA. I don't know. Nothing got through to him, nothing reached his heart! Obviously nothing can soil his sacred fire. I knelt on the ground . . . he just doesn't understand . . .

YELENA. I told you to wait! You should have let me speak to him first.

MELANIA. I thought you'd let me down. I offered him everything – all my money, the price I sold my soul for, my

abused spirit – and he wouldn't accept it! Who else would
have done that? No-one but him.

PROTASOV (*enters, carrying his hat*). Yelena, a bath, quick! Take
everything off and fling it in the stove! Fima! A bath, please!
Damn that Fima, she's some sort of myth, she's no maid,
that's for sure.

YELENA. Don't make such a fuss. The bath's ready, and I'll do
the rest myself.

PROTASOV. Go on, quickly, please! Cholera's no joke.

YELENA (*exiting*). I'm going, I'm going.

> PROTASOV *sees his wife out, surreptitiously watching* MELANIA.
> *She is sitting, her head bowed, looking guilty.*

PROTASOV (*re-entering*). Hm, yes . . . it's rather overcast today,
not a very pleasant afternoon.

MELANIA (*quietly*). No.

PROTASOV. No. And this cholera . . . well, it couldn't have
come at a worse time.

MELANIA. Indeed, and so suddenly.

PROTASOV. On top of that, the refrigerator's broken down.

MELANIA. Pavel Fyodorovich, forgive me!

PROTASOV (*warily*). Er . . . what for? What exactly do you
mean?

MELANIA. Forget everything – everything I said to you, forget it!

PROTASOV (*delighted*). No, are you serious?

MELANIA. Yes. I've been so stupid. Shameless.

PROTASOV. Melania Nikolaevna . . . I'm very fond of you . . .
I mean, I respect you – you're a wonderfully spontaneous
person, so dedicated. You take such a lively interest in
everything, but, well . . . it's too much . . . I mean, all those

things you said, we can't! Let's be good friends, and leave it at that. We should all be friends, shouldn't we?

MELANIA. I'm ashamed to look at you.

PROTASOV. Oh, never mind that. Give me your hand. There, that's splendid! No, people are wonderful, truly. They're so simple, yet so intelligent, with such a marvellous facility for understanding one another. I love people, I really do – they're amazingly interesting creatures!

MELANIA (*smiling*). I've never seen people like that. I lived amongst shopkeepers – my husband sold meat. It was only in this house I saw real persons . . . and immediately tried to buy one.

PROTASOV. What did you say?

MELANIA. Don't listen to me. It's just how I am.

PROTASOV (*animatedly*). Look, tell you what – why don't we have some tea?

MELANIA. Yes, fine. I'll go through to Yelena Nikolaevna's room – get tidied up a bit.

PROTASOV. Meanwhile, I'll organise the tea! Our refrigerator's broken down, you know, damn the thing. And Yegor's wife's ill, so there's no-one to fix it, which means I can't work today.

PROTASOV *exits laughing to his own room.* MELANIA *watches him go, filled with emotion.*

MELANIA. Oh, my darling child! My own beautiful baby!

Exits to YELENA's *room.* ANTONOVNA *enters from the dining-room, annoyed, muttering.*

ANTONOVNA. You'd think the Mongol hordes had passed through here! Just look at it! Things scattered all over the place, a shambles! Can't leave them for two seconds! It's only dead folk as are tidy – in the graveyard. That's the only place you'll get any peace.

LIZA *and* CHEPURNOY *enter from the veranda.*

Liza dear, your medicine and milk.

LIZA (*irritated*). Oh, be quiet – go away.

ANTONOVNA. Well, really! (*Exits.*)

CHEPURNOY. So . . . it's all over?

LIZA. Yes, Boris, it is. Not another word about it, not ever!

CHEPURNOY. All right. But the reason I mentioned it today was that I thought you were making a mistake.

LIZA. No! It's not my illness that's preventing me. I'm not afraid of it. But I can't . . . I don't want to have children. Doesn't anyone ever ask themselves what people are born for? Well, I've asked myself. And there's no room on this earth for a personal life, for anyone without the strength to make all life on earth their own. Anyway, you'll go away, yes?

CHEPURNOY (*calmly*). All right.

VAGHIN *enters from the veranda.*

LIZA. It'll be easier for you. And don't wear red ties, they're so vulgar! Honestly, today of all days, and you're in a red tie, it's such a pity.

VAGHIN. What a day! It's like October.

CHEPURNOY. Yes, it's turned out pretty nasty.

LIZA. Where are you thinking of going?

CHEPURNOY. Me? Mogilev province – to a better place, I hope.

LIZA (*alarmed*). Where? Why did you say that?

CHEPURNOY. What, Mogilev? I have a lot of friends there.

VAGHIN. No – a better place. That's what people say in fun about the dead.

LIZA (*shudders*). That's enough!

VAGHIN. It's only a joke, you're not frightened, surely? You don't think Boris Nikolaevich is going to die? Not unless he shoots himself.

LIZA (*reproachfully*). Why do you say these things?

VAGHIN. Let me hasten to reassure you – I don't know of any case of a vet shooting himself.

ANTONOVNA (*from the dining-room*). Liza dear, come and pour the tea.

LIZA *silently exits.*

VAGHIN. It's sinful of me, I know, but I do love teasing her. She makes a parade of her sorrow for the world. They really are frightful bores, these people who take on all the world's woes. And I have a pathological aversion to any kind of sickness.

CHEPURNOY. What about that picture – 'Walking Towards the Sun' or whatever it's called – are you going to paint it?

VAGHIN. Oh, absolutely! It's a magnificent subject, *n'est-ce pas?* I shall want to use you for it, by the way.

CHEPURNOY (*surprised*). Me? Where are you going to put me? On the ship's bottom?

VAGHIN (*peering closely at him*). You have a very stubborn-looking frown-line, I think, above the eyes . . . full of character! You don't mind if I try and capture it?

CHEPURNOY. Go ahead.

VAGHIN (*takes out his sketch-pad*). That's a luxury . . . I won't take a minute. (*Draws.*)

CHEPURNOY. Do you like jokes?

VAGHIN. Love them. As long as they're not too silly.

CHEPURNOY. Right – I'll tell you one.

VAGHIN. Please do. But I never talk while I'm drawing.

CHEPURNOY. Yes, so I can hear. Anyway, here goes . . . There was this English diplomatic mission, crossing the Channel from Dover to Calais, and there was a Frenchman on board, and they started bragging about who were the better, the French or the English. And the Englishmen said, 'Look at us, we get everywhere!' And the Frenchman said, 'No, you don't – lots of our diplomats have been drowned in these waters, but not a single English one!' At which point a young English diplomat jumped over the side – plop! – and promptly drowned!

VAGHIN (*after a pause*). And then?

CHEPURNOY. Well, that's it.

VAGHIN. The whole story?

CHEPURNOY. Yes. What more do you want? The man wanted to uphold the honour of his country, so he drowned himself!

VAGHIN. Hm – it's a joke, I suppose, but it's not very funny.

CHEPURNOY. Your tie's very nicely tied.

VAGHIN. D'you like it? A certain lady taught me that.

CHEPURNOY. It's a nice colour too.

PROTASOV (*enters*). What's this – drawing? Hasn't Lena appeared yet? You know, Dmitri, she's been fussing around a cholera patient today.

VAGHIN. What?

PROTASOV. Yes, it's true! My blacksmith's wife. What do you think of that?

VAGHIN. Well, it's unwise, to say the least. Why did you allow her?

YELENA (*emerging from her room*). I surely don't have to be *allowed* to do anything.

VAGHIN. But it isn't any of your business!

YELENA. Why not? If I want to make it my business, well . . .

VAGHIN. But you've been . . . oh, God knows!

PROTASOV. No, I think she's done splendidly! I was a bit afraid for her, I must confess. You did take your drops, didn't you?

VAGHIN (*finishes his drawing*). Right, that's it. Thank you very much! That's a wonderful feature, that little frown-line of yours.

CHEPURNOY. I'm so pleased.

LIZA (*from the dining-room*). Come and have some tea!

VAGHIN. Coming! (*Takes CHEPURNOY's arm, and they exit.*)

PROTASOV (*sotto voce*). Lena, I've something to tell you . . .

YELENA. What, now?

PROTASOV (*hurriedly*). Yes! You know, something ridiculous has happened! Melania Nikolaevna – has she gone?

YELENA (*smiling*). Yes, she's gone.

PROTASOV: Lena, please – don't laugh! I think she's fallen in love with me. Common or garden love, would you believe? How d'you like that? I mean, honest to God, I gave her no encouragement, Lena . . . what are you laughing at? You've got to take this seriously. It's really unpleasant, you've no idea! She was crying right here, kissing my trousers, and my hand, this one . . .

YELENA (*laughing*). Oh, stop it, Pavel.

PROTASOV (*slightly annoyed*). You astonish me! She's absolutely serious, I tell you. She offered to give me all her money. I want to live with you, she says! She calls me 'darling', no less! And please don't think I gave her any cause to do that. And she stinks of saltpetre, God knows why . . . what's the matter with you?

YELENA (*laughing*). I can't help it . . . it's funny . . . you're funny!

PROTASOV (*offended*). What d'you mean? This is serious, it isn't funny, it's absurd! I was scared stiff. I tried to say something to her, but my head was in a complete muddle. She's deadly serious, you know. Oh yes, and she told me you knew all about it, but about what exactly, I hadn't a clue. I didn't even want to mention it to you at first.

YELENA (*gently*). I do know all about it . . . you dear, sweet man.

PROTASOV. You know? But how . . . Well, why didn't you warn me?

YELENA (*as if remembering something – coldly*). Let's leave it until this evening.

PROTASOV. Yes, all right. I'd like some tea. Anyway, if you do know, I'm glad! And you'll sort all this out, right?

LIZA (*from the dining-room*). Lena! Come on.

YELENA. I'm coming.

PROTASOV. So, you'll see to all that, will you?

YELENA. Yes, yes, don't worry! Now, come on . . .

They walk towards the door.

PROTASOV. You know, when I lifted her up from the floor, her armpits . . . (*Whispers the remainder.*)

YELENA. Ugh! Pavel, you're disgusting.

The stage is empty a few moments. Conversation and crockery noises from the dining-room. CHEPURNOY *emerges.*

CHEPURNOY. Well, I can have a smoke here.

He crosses to the window, his hands behind his back. He takes his cigarette from his mouth, looks at it, and begins softly singing.

'All that night lay a golden cloud . . . ' (*His voice trembles and breaks off.*) Ahem . . . 'All that night lay a golden cloud . . . '

VAGHIN (*enters*). 'On the breast of the giant's mighty crag . . . ' They've flung me out too – not allowed to smoke.

CHEPURNOY. So, you like funny stories?

VAGHIN. You have another bad joke?

CHEPURNOY. I'll make one up for you. Meanwhile, I'd better be off home.

VAGHIN. When will I hear the joke, then?

CHEPURNOY. Tomorrow! It's raining. (*In a cod accent.*) Now, then – me brolly, or not me brolly, as Prince Hamlet says. Well, goodbye!

VAGHIN (*catches him by the arm*). I take it you're going somewhere?

CHEPURNOY (*smiling*). Yes, I am. Got to go.

VAGHIN (*also smiling*). Ah, well – *bon voyage*! I don't know why, but I've taken a great liking to you today.

CHEPURNOY. Thank you.

VAGHIN. You look like a lover today. Tell me, have you ever been in love?

CHEPURNOY. Well, when I was a student, I had a crush on my landlady. I even told her about it.

VAGHIN. Was she beautiful?

CHEPURNOY. It's hard to say. She was all of fifty at the time.
And when I made my declaration of love, she put my rent up
by three roubles a month.

VAGHIN (*laughing*). Seriously?

CHEPURNOY. Yes, indeed. Anyway, goodbye!

Laughing, he exits to the dining-room. VAGHIN *watches him go, deep
in thought, then begins pacing around the room, smoking, humming a
tune, and shaking his head from time to time.* ANTONOVNA *enters
from* YELENA's *bedroom.*

ANTONOVNA (*muttering*). Hm – I thought it was him still
hanging around.

VAGHIN. Who?

ANTONOVNA. The Ukrainian. Where is he?

VAGHIN. He's gone home.

ANTONOVNA. That's him all over – comes here, has his tea,
clears off. And there's that poor girl, she's fair worn out, can't
even sleep nights. You could at least've told him . . .

VAGHIN. What girl are you talking about? Why can't she sleep?
What are we supposed to say to her?

ANTONOVNA. Now, come off it, sir – there's only one girl in
the house. Getting on in years, too. What's the point of
alarming her? She's sick enough as it is. But you lot just stroll
around, talking non-stop, and you don't care there's a person
here so downright miserable, she might even do away with
herself!

Exits to the dining-room. VAGHIN *rubs his forehead vigorously, deep
in thought, then shakes his head as if he has reached some decision.*

VAGHIN. Pavel!

PROTASOV (*entering with a book in his hand*). Yes, I'm here.

VAGHIN (*distastefully*). You know, you look really smug!

PROTASOV (*surprised*). Is that what you called me in to tell me?

VAGHIN. We need to have a talk.

PROTASOV (*yawns*). Uhuh. Everybody wants a talk with me today. I've already heard a few strange things, and not one word of sense.

VAGHIN. Well, I have something sensible to say.

PROTASOV (*looks at his book*). I wouldn't bet on it.

VAGHIN. Put your book down.

PROTASOV. Where? Or why, rather?

VAGHIN. Put it down. Look – the point is . . . I love Yelena.

PROTASOV (*calmly*). Now there's a surprise! Who doesn't love her?

VAGHIN. No, I'm in love with her, don't you understand? As a woman.

PROTASOV. So? (*As if on a sudden thought, leaps to his feet.*) But . . . but what about her? Does she know? Have you told her? What does she say?

VAGHIN. Yes, she knows.

PROTASOV. Well? Did she give you an answer?

VAGHIN (*uncomfortably*). No, nothing definite . . . not yet.

PROTASOV (*pleased*). Well, of course! I knew she wouldn't, it goes without saying.

VAGHIN (*restrained*). Now, hold on . . . Actually, the fact is – you've been treating her abominably.

PROTASOV (*startled*). I have? How? When?

VAGHIN. You don't pay her any attention. You've killed her love for you.

PROTASOV (*alarmed*). Is that what she says?

VAGHIN. It's what I say.

PROTASOV (*offended*). Now look here, sir! What's the matter with you all today – has everybody gone crazy? One says I don't love Lena, another one says she doesn't love me – what on earth's going on? This is utterly irresponsible – you'll end up driving me mad, all of you! And she's keeping quiet, she's not saying a word! What are you all up to? Oh, I don't understand any of this!

VAGHIN. Pavel, you and I have been friends since childhood. I'm very fond of you . . .

PROTASOV. Well, try adding a little tact to your fondness, if you can. Yes, do! And allow a man the right to speak up for himself, to stand up for his freedom, his dignity. When he can do that, he'll do it better than you . . .

VAGHIN. And if he can't?

PROTASOV. Then to hell with him! He's not a man then, is he?

VAGHIN. Supposing he doesn't want to?

PROTASOV. That's impossible. I'm sorry, Dmitri, but you're like all these artists, you're just not serious. Not a word out of you as late as yesterday, now suddenly today it's: 'I'm in love with her!'

VAGHIN. I can't talk to you. Anyway, I've said what had to be said. I'm leaving.

PROTASOV. No, hold on . . . I'll call Lena . . . Lena!

VAGHIN (*alarmed*). What are you doing? What's this for?

PROTASOV. What for? Lena! I want her to tell me what's going on, with you here. Lena, please! (YELENA *emerges from her room.*) Oh, there you are, Yelena. Well, now, it seems he's in love too, just like Melania. Yes, indeed! Only, it's you he's in love with . . .

YELENA, *unsmiling, looks questioningly at* VAGHIN.

VAGHIN (*excitedly*). Well, why not? I told him I loved you, and that you're unhappy with him.

YELENA. Why, thank you – that's very gallant of you – well done!

VAGHIN (*offended*). I don't deserve your sarcasm. I don't want to feel any enmity towards Pavel, but it's arisen, I can't help it. All right, I've acted stupidly, I've been tactless and rude, but I was motivated by feelings of friendship, and love. I gave into an impulse – something the nanny said put it into my mind. I just wanted something . . . oh, I don't know, something better for you, Yelena. And between people like us, well, everything ought to be clear and straightforward.

YELENA. Thank you.

PROTASOV. I didn't say anything to offend you, did I, Dmitri?

VAGHIN. No! Anyway, I'd better go. Goodbye . . .

YELENA. You'll come tomorrow?

VAGHIN (*exits*). Yes, probably.

PROTASOV (*looks questioningly at his wife*). Well, Lena? What now? How do you see all this?

YELENA. What about you?

PROTASOV. It's a good thing you're so calm. Whew! What a day! Did he make some sort of declaration to you?

YELENA. Yes, he did.

PROTASOV. Told you he loved you, and so forth?

YELENA. Especially the so forth.

PROTASOV. Well, really – these artists! So, what did you say to him?

YELENA. Lots of things . . . various things.

PROTASOV. But you did tell him you loved me?

YELENA. No, I didn't say that.

PROTASOV. Well, that's a pity. You should've told him . . . you should've told him right off: I love Pavel, he's my husband! After that, well, it goes without saying, he would have . . . hm . . . yes! Actually, I'm not sure how he would've behaved in that event. Anyway, it's not important.

YELENA. So, what do you think is important?

PROTASOV. Well, that an incident like that shouldn't be repeated.

YELENA. Pavel! You've talked about him, you've even tried to make his mind up for him. You've stated your wish not to be upset like this again . . . Now where does all that leave me?

PROTASOV (*anxiously*). In what way? What do you mean?

YELENA. Not much. I feel you don't really need me. I've never played any part in your life. You're so remote from me, a stranger. Who am I to you? You never ask how I live my life, what I think . . .

PROTASOV. Never ask? But . . . well, I don't have time for conversation, Lena! And why didn't you say something yourself?

YELENA (*proudly*). I'm not going to ask you, like a beggar, for something I should have by right, as your wife, as a human being. I can't ask, and I would never demand. What's the point of force?

PROTASOV (*despairingly*). Oh, damn, damn, this is so difficult! These disagreements are so unnecessary – all these rows, they're so offensive!

YELENA. Don't get excited. Actually, I've decided to leave you. I've made a firm decision, and in my mind, I've already said goodbye to you.

PROTASOV (*amazed*). Lena – no! Where would you go? Why? You . . . you love Dmitri? Yes? Is that it?

YELENA. No. I don't want to marry him, if that's what you mean.

PROTASOV (*delightedly*). Then that's fine! But you no longer love me, is that it? Tell me! Quickly, Lena!

YELENA. Why should you care?

PROTASOV (*sincerely*). I do love you, you know.

YELENA. Oh, stop it, Pavel.

PROTASOV (*doggedly*). Lena, my word of honour! I just never have the time. Listen, this isn't serious, surely? I can see you've been hurt, and I'm sorry, forgive me, Lena – forgive and forget, eh? I mean, if you leave, I'll keep wondering where you are, how you're doing – and then what'll happen to my work? You'll be crippling me, Lena . . . really, what about my work? It'll be either work, or else think about you . . .

YELENA (*bitterly*). Just listen to yourself – examine what you're saying: not one word about me, note – not a single word!

PROTASOV (*falling to his knees*). What d'you mean, not a word? Lena, I'm telling you I can't live without you! All right, it's all my fault – forgive me, please! But don't stop me living, Lena – life's too short, and there's so much fascinating work to be done!

YELENA. And what about me? What does life hold for me? (*Stops to listen.*) Wait . . .

A loud clatter of footsteps hurrying downstairs. PROTASOV *leaps to his feet in alarm.* LIZA *rushes in, wide-eyed with terror. Her lips move, she tries to make signs with her hands, but she can't speak.*

PROTASOV. Liza! What's the matter?

YELENA. Water! Give her some water!

LIZA. No! Listen to me . . . something terrible has happened. Believe me, I know. Such pain, suddenly . . . as if my heart had stopped! Some terrible thing, somewhere . . . someone close to us . . .

YELENA. Liza, stop, calm down. You're imagining things . . .

LIZA (*shrieks*). No, no – you've got to believe me! (*Falls into* PROTASOV's *arms.*)

Curtain.

Act Four

The setting is the same as for Act Two. Midday. Lunch is over, and coffee has been served. ROMAN, wearing a red shirt, is repairing the garden fence. LUSHA is standing by the veranda, watching him. PROTASOV is heard laughing indoors.

LUSHA. Where are you from?

ROMAN. Ryazan.

LUSHA. Really? I'm from Kaluga.

ROMAN. So what?

LUSHA. You're right scary, you are.

ROMAN (*grins*). What, me? Scary? Must be the beard, eh? Nah, think nothing of it. I'm a widower. Time I got married again.

LUSHA (*goes closer to him*). Is it true, what they were saying in the shop, that the master's a sorcerer?

ROMAN. Could be. They're clever folk, the gentry.

LUSHA. I'm scared of them. They're terrible kind, all lovey-dovey – not like gentry at all!

ROMAN. And then there's some of them as makes counterfeit money.

LUSHA. Really?

ROMAN. Yes, nothing to it. They get hard labour for it, though.

PROTASOV *and* LIZA *emerge from the house.*

PROTASOV. Now, this is splendid! Drink up your milk, Liza.

LIZA (*wearily, making a face*). Why is that man wearing a red shirt?

PROTASOV. Because he likes it. You know, Lena's a wonderful woman, so clever . . .

LIZA (*stirring her milk with a spoon*). Really?

PROTASOV (*pacing up and down the veranda*). Yes, Liza, yes indeed! Believe me. Ah, you must be the new maid – well, well. What's your name?

LUSHA (*shyly*). Me? Lukeria.

PROTASOV. Aha . . . Lukeria . . . hm! So, can you read?

LUSHA. No, sir. But I can say my prayers.

PROTASOV. And . . . er . . . um . . . are you married?

LUSHA. Not yet, sir. I'm still only young.

PROTASOV. So, you've come straight from the country, then?

LUSHA. Yes, sir. From my village.

PROTASOV. Good, good. Well, you'll be staying here with us. We're quite ordinary people. You'll enjoy yourself here, you know.

LUSHA *exits*.

LIZA (*smiling*). You're always so funny, Pavel.

PROTASOV. Funny? D'you think so? Actually, Liza, that's what Lena says too. I suppose you're right. In point of fact, we're pretty remote from the ordinary people. We need to do something, we must get them to come closer to us somehow. Yelena was just talking about that, very eloquently – so simply and convincingly. I'm very struck – such a wealth of intelligence, and real heart, right here beside me, and I didn't know! I didn't even know how to benefit from it. There's obviously something deep down stupid about me, something limited.

LIZA. Oh, stop it. You just don't take any notice of people.

PROTASOV. Yes, that's right. You have a point. Last night, you know, after we'd put you to bed, Lena and I sat talking for three whole hours. Then we . . . er . . . then we sent for Dmitri. You know he . . . er . . . oh dear, we shouldn't talk about that.

LIZA. About what?

PROTASOV. Well, actually . . . Dmitri's supposed to have fallen in love with Yelena. At least he says he has. But I don't believe him, and neither does she. Yelena was quite magnificent, the way she spoke to him – you know, like a very intelligent, loving mother. It was really quite moving, we were all in tears. You know, Liza, life's so easy and pleasant if people just try to understand and respect one another, yes! We'll be friends now, all three of us.

LIZA (*bitterly*). Three? What about me?

PROTASOV. And you, of course! Obviously, you too. We'll all be friends, Liza, and we'll work, we'll build up a great treasury of thoughts and feelings for all people, and we'll be able to take pride in the knowledge that we've done so much important and necessary work for them, so that when we depart this life, we'll do so pleasantly tired, and calm, completely reconciled to the necessity of our going. That's such a wonderful thing, Liza! So clear and simple!

LIZA. I love it when you talk like that. I love you, and life seems to me just the way you describe it – so simple, and beautiful. But when I'm alone . . . and I'm always alone . . .

PROTASOV. Don't be sad, Liza, eh? Yesterday you were imagining things, but you're ill, Liza, it was just your poor nerves.

LIZA (*fearfully*). Don't talk to me about illness! Don't, please! Let me forget it. I must, it's vital! That's enough. I want to live too. I have a right to live!

PROTASOV. Liza, don't get excited. (*YELENA enters.*) Ah, here's Lena. This is my Lena, my very good, and slightly forbidding, severe friend . . .

YELENA. Don't, please. That's enough. (*Indicates* LIZA *with a glance.*)

LIZA (*nervously*). Yelena! You do love him, don't you?

YELENA (*embarrassed*). Yes, of course I do.

LIZA. Oh, I'm so glad! I thought you . . .

YELENA. It's been hard for me at times, terribly hard. You know, this gentleman here – without realising, and certainly without wishing to – can be so hurtful.

LIZA (*excitedly*). No, wait, wait! I know, too . . . I'm in love with Boris Nikolaevich. Yesterday I refused him, turned him down flat! And later that night I suddenly had this feeling, that something had happened to him, some sort of accident, something terrible! And he's so close to me, closer than any of you! Yesterday I realised that I do love him. I need him . . . I can't live without him!

NAZAR (*shouts somewhere outside*). Roman!

ROMAN (*quietly*). What?

LIZA. Oh, he's so stubborn! But he is wonderful, isn't he?

YELENA (*kissing her*). Liza, dearest . . . I wish you every happiness. We all need a little happiness in our lives.

LIZA. Lena, your lips are burning.

PROTASOV. Anyway – congratulations! This'll work wonders for you, you'll see! Yes, indeed – a normal life, that's absolutely crucial! And Chepurnoy – yes, I like him! He's so much cleverer than his sister, there's no comparison.

NAZAR (*shouts*). Roman, damn you!

ROMAN. I said, what d'you want?

LIZA. I feel at peace now. We'll go away into the steppes somewhere – he loves the steppe country. And we'll be alone, just the two of us, walking through the green wilderness, and we'll be able to see everything around us – everything and nothing!

NAZAR (*emerging round the corner of the house*). Roman! Was I calling you or wasn't I?

ROMAN. I can hear you – what d'you want?

NAZAR. You idle lump! Go and shut the gates – and the wicket, too. Ah, Mr Protasov, my respects to you, sir – how are you?

PROTASOV. Splendid, thank you! What are you shutting the gates for?

NAZAR. What, haven't you heard, sir? There's a bit of unrest among folks, on account of that there sickness. The way they sees it, there's no sickness at all – they're saying it's the doctors making it all up, to do more business, like.

PROTASOV. What nonsense, that's ridiculous!

NAZAR. Well, of course, sir, but that's folks for you. That's why they call 'em the vulgar herd, right? They'll dream up all sorts, they will, out of their ignorance. There's too many doctors, they say, they've got no work, so they go and . . . Well, anyway, just in case, to keep the place safe, and for a bit of peace, like, I've told 'em to lock the gates.

PROTASOV. Oh, honestly, this kind of nonsense could only happen here!

NAZAR. You don't need to tell me, sir. Why, just yesterday they gave one of them doctors a right going-over.

LIZA. Who? What was his name, do you know?

NAZAR. No, ma'am.

YELENA. Liza, what's the matter? Boris isn't a doctor.

LIZA. No . . . he's not a doctor.

YELENA. Let's go in. (*Leads* LIZA *into the house.*)

NAZAR. Gave the young lady a bit of a fright there. Mr
Protasov, sir – didn't Mr Chepurnoy say anything to you?

MISHA *appears from around the corner.*

MISHA. Dad! Dad! That's the builder just come! (*To*
PROTASOV.) Good day, your honour!

PROTASOV. Good day.

NAZAR. And I'll just say, sir – till the next time! (*Exits.*)

MISHA. It's a nice day, not too hot.

PROTASOV. Yes, it's quite nice.

MISHA. Sir, if I might enquire – that young woman who was
working here – Fima . . . Has she left?

PROTASOV. Yes, she has.

MISHA. They say she's getting married – to some rich man,
would that be right?

PROTASOV. I've no idea. How should I know?

MISHA. So what was she like? Was she a decent girl?

PROTASOV. Oh, undoubtedly. A bit . . . um . . . clumsy, that's
all. Broke a lot of dishes.

MISHA. No, really? Hm . . . Anyway, sir, my old dad didn't say
anything to you about a chemical works, did he?

PROTASOV (*surprised*). A chemical works? No. What are we
talking about, exactly?

MISHA. Well, we've had this idea, you see, to build a chemical
plant and hire you as manager.

PROTASOV. I'm sorry? What d'you mean, hire? I'm not some
clodhopper, you know. You have a rather odd way of
expressing yourself.

MISHA. I beg your pardon, sir! Anyway, the matter's not in the words, sir – it goes deeper than that. Me and my old dad, you see, we've got the greatest respect for you, sir.

PROTASOV (*drily*). I'm deeply touched.

MISHA. I mean, your finances aren't exactly a secret, sir, and we know you'll soon be looking out for some sort of government job. And that's hard work, sir, the more so for the likes of yourself . . .

PROTASOV. Hm, yes. You may be right.

MISHA. Anyway, my old dad and me, being appreciative, like, of your capabilities and knowledge, and seeing as you'd be a pretty handy man for the company, well, we've decided to make you this proposition, sir: you draw up an estimate for the equipping of a factory . . .

PROTASOV. No, look, I'm sorry, I've absolutely no idea how to do an estimate, I've never done anything like that! And industrial chemistry doesn't interest me. I'm most grateful to you for the compliment, but . . .

MISHA. What, you're not interested in technology?

PROTASOV. Dear me, no, it's extremely boring. Not my cup of tea at all.

MISHA (*looks at him pityingly*). Are you serious, sir?

PROTASOV. Absolutely.

MISHA. That's a shame. Still, the way I see it, sir . . . you're going to have to change your mind. Anyway, goodbye for now, sir!

He exits. YELENA *emerges from the house.*

YELENA (*alarmed*). Pavel . . .

PROTASOV. What is it?

YELENA. Liza's ill – I think it's serious.

PROTASOV. Oh, she's always like that after an attack, it's nothing. D'you know, I've just been talking with that . . . whatsisname . . . the landlord's son . . . A thoroughly unprepossessing chap, but would you believe, he showed a really touching concern for me? Put it rather crudely, it's true, but even so . . . He's suggesting I draw up some sort of estimate, and just generally . . .

YELENA. Just generally wants to make use of you, as an instrument to enrich himself. Yes, I know all about their plans, the old man was speaking to me. What's the matter, are you cold?

PROTASOV. Me? No, not at all.

YELENA. Why have you put on your galoshes, then?

PROTASOV (*looks down at his feet*). Good heavens – galoshes! When did I put them on? That's odd – I honestly don't know how I . . .

YELENA. Possibly the new maid put them out for you, and you didn't notice.

PROTASOV. That's right – oh God, please don't let her come near me – she scares me, she's so rough – she'll break all my equipment, or spill something. I caught her this morning pouring hydrogen peroxide over her head; she obviously thought it was eau-de-cologne. (*Takes* YELENA *by the hand.*) Darling Lena, you really put me through it yesterday – that was torture.

YELENA. For a few minutes? You've tortured me for months . . . years . . .

PROTASOV. Please, don't . . .

YELENA. If you only knew, how humiliating it is to love, and never to feel *your* love! You made a beggar out of me, made me sit waiting to be noticed, waiting for a kind word or a caress. That's so hurtful! You have such a radiant spirit, that dear, sweet head of yours is full of great things, but very little of the greatest of all things – people!

PROTASOV. Lena, that's all in the past! That's over and done with. The only thing is . . . well, Dmitri . . . Of course, I feel sorry for him, but . . . There's someone ringing the bell . . . oh, and the gates are locked! It's probably Dmitri, though I'd rather it were Chepurnoy, for Liza's sake, naturally.

YELENA (*mischievously*). For Liza's sake? Really?

PROTASOV. Oh, come on, Lena, you surely don't suspect me of jealousy, and all that?

YELENA (*solemnly*). Oh no, of course not. You? You, for whom nothing except science . . .

PROTASOV. Lena, what if I were to give you a smack, eh?

He is about to kiss her, then sees MELANIA *walking towards the veranda. He is embarrassed, and distracted.*

Well, look at that, Lena, you've got a feather or something on your shoulder.

MELANIA (*with a guilty smile*). Good day.

PROTASOV (*exaggeratedly pleased*). Melania Nikolaevna! You . . . um . . . we haven't seen you for ages!

MELANIA. What d'you mean ages? I was here yesterday – have you forgotten already?

PROTASOV. Yes, that's right! No, of course I remember!

MELANIA. I thought you were having a laugh at me, because of yesterday.

PROTASOV (*hastily*). Oh, good heavens, no! No, that was just silly. (*Tries to correct himself.*) Um . . . what I mean is . . . well, it could happen to anybody. (*Finally gives up.*)

YELENA. You'd be better to say nothing, Pavel.

MELANIA (*lovingly*). Oh, you're so . . .

PAVEL. Hm, yes . . . I'll keep quiet. I'll go indoors, take off my galoshes. God knows why I've got them on.

MELANIA (*sadly, laughing*). You see? Just silly, he says. I opened up my heart to him . . . it could happen to anybody, he says . . . as if I'd stepped on his corn!

YELENA. Melania, don't take offence.

MELANIA (*sincerely*). Oh, my dear! Me, take offence at him? I haven't slept a wink all night, pacing up and down the house, thinking: how *could* I have dared to speak to him that way? You know what it was, don't you. I had this idea, you see – I could attract him with money! Yes, who can resist a large sum of money? That's what I thought. But he wasn't tempted.

YELENA. Forget all that. (LIZA *enters slowly*.) What is it, Liza?

LIZA (*lifelessly*). Boris isn't here?

YELENA. No, not yet. He hasn't come.

LIZA. No . . . (*Goes back into the house.*)

MELANIA. She didn't say hello to me. And she looks so pale!

YELENA. She had an attack yesterday.

MELANIA. Again? Poor thing. Anyway, you're telling me to forget, but I won't forget! I mustn't. If I forget, I'll end up doing something stupid again. Yes, my darling! Oh, what a horrible old bag I am! Brazen, utterly corrupt. I don't have many thoughts, and what I do have . . . well, they're not straight, they're like worms, wriggling in all directions. And I don't want thoughts like that, I don't! I want to be honest, and decent. I've got to be! Otherwise I can do so much harm.

YELENA. If you want to, then you will be! You've had such a hard, ugly life. You need to relax now, forget the past.

MELANIA. Yes, it's been hard. God knows it has! I've had my share of beatings, but it's not my back or my face I feel sorry for – it's my soul! My soul's been wrenched out of shape, my heart's been soiled, dirtied. I can't believe in anything good, it's so difficult for me, but without that belief, what sort of life is it? Look at Boris – he laughs at everything, he believes in nothing, but what is he? He's like a stray dog. But you believed me straightaway. I was astonished. I thought you were making a fool of me, but you were so kind and affectionate, trying to explain me to myself.

YELENA. That's enough now, my dear.

MELANIA. And you did it so well, so simply. It's true – it isn't me, the woman, that loves him, it's me the human being. I hadn't ever felt the human being in me before. I didn't believe in it.

YELENA. I'm so glad you understood.

MELANIA. I did, I understood right away. But even so, I thought, let's try, let's see if I can purchase this amusing gentleman to be my husband. That's how low I've sunk!

YELENA. Don't speak like that about yourself. You've got to respect yourself, otherwise life's just impossible. Oh, I feel like giving you a hug.

MELANIA. Yes, do, please! For the love of Christ, give alms to the rich tradeswoman . . .

YELENA. Melania, don't! You mustn't! And please don't cry.

MELANIA. It doesn't matter, let me wash out my heart. Yelena Nikolaevna, please – take me in. Teach me something good, something fine. You're so clever, you can . . . (LIZA enters.) Lizaveta, how are you?

LIZA (silently gives her her hand). He hasn't come yet, Yelena?

YELENA. No. What's wrong?

LIZA. No?

YELENA. Are you feeling ill?

LIZA. No, just sad. No! (*Exits to the garden.*)

MELANIA. Who is she waiting for?

YELENA. Your brother Boris. You know they're engaged?

MELANIA. Good heavens! So that means I'll be related to
Pavel? And to you? Oh, Boris . . . and Liza, the darling! I'll
go and see her – may I?

YELENA. Of course.

MELANIA (*animatedly, overjoyed*). Now, look how everything's
working out! This is wonderful – let me give you a kiss!
(ANTONOVNA *emerges from the house.*) I'll go and see her, in
the garden. Hello, Nanny, hello, my dear! (*Exits.*)

ANTONOVNA. Hello. What's that stupid creature up to – that
new maid – why doesn't she clear the table? Taking on a
maid through an agency – you've got to hire them yourself,
not through an agency!

YELENA (*takes her by the shoulders*). Nanny, stop fussing – it's such
a lovely day.

ANTONOVNA. It's summer, you've got to have warm days.
And you've got to have a bit of order, any time of the year.
That new girl sits down for her tea, and she empties a whole
samovar, she does, all by herself – she's like a horse!

VAGHIN *enters.*

YELENA. You don't begrudge her the water?

ANTONOVNA. Indeed I don't. But she crunches up the sugar,
like it was turnip or something, yes. (*Picks something up from the
table and goes into the house.*)

YELENA. *Bonjour, mon chevalier.*

VAGHIN (*embarrassed*). May I kiss your hand?

YELENA. Why ever not?

VAGHIN (*sighs*). Well, you know . . .

YELENA. And such a deep sigh. Oh, you poor martyr.

VAGHIN (*stung*). I'm looking at you now, and d'you know what's just come into my mind?

YELENA. No, I wonder what? Tell me.

VAGHIN. That you made use of me, to get Pavel to favour you with a little of his attention. Yes, a neat trick.

YELENA. *Mon chevalier*! Your tone of voice . . . 'You made use of me . . .' What sort of talk is that? 'A neat trick . . .'

VAGHIN (*bitterly*). You've taught me a lesson, like a naughty boy.

YELENA (*seriously*). Dmitri Sergeyevich, I don't like listening to nonsense.

VAGHIN (*after some thought, simply*). I feel I've been playing a part of some kind, not a very clever one, and that hurts me. In fact, I don't feel too good at all, after yesterday's conversation, something's not right in my mind. Yelena Nikolaevna, will you tell me the truth?

YELENA. Do you really have to ask that?

VAGHIN. I want to ask you: were you never attracted to me?

YELENA. As a man – no, never. As a human being – I love you very deeply.

VAGHIN (*laughing*). And I'm supposed to be flattered by that? I don't understand people, I really don't. As for me, I love the whole of you – all of you at once! It struck me yesterday, and I realised that the woman and the human being are so completely fused together, so indissolubly linked, in one beautiful, rounded totality . . . that I felt ashamed, and sorry for myself. And yesterday I fell in love with you.

YELENA (*annoyed*). Oh, not again . . . why?

VAGHIN (*simply and insistently*). Yes, I fell in love! For good! And I'm not asking anything of you. I'll probably get married, make a suitable match, and so forth, but I'll go on loving you, I'll always love you! Anyway, I've said my piece. You're fed up with me, aren't you.

YELENA (*holds out her hand to him*). I believe you. I think you're telling the truth.

VAGHIN. What about before? You never felt there was any truth in what I said? No?

YELENA (*with a faint smile*). No, never. And how did this happen, do you think? I couldn't help myself once, and complained to you about feeling lonely. You were wonderful to me, so straightforward and open, so pure! I began to have such a warm feeling of gratitude towards you, and it was at that point – then and only then, notice – that you started talking about love.

VAGHIN. Only then? And did that offend you?

YELENA (*smiling*). I don't know. A little, perhaps.

VAGHIN (*sadly, a little annoyed*). No, I'm no genius, to put it mildly. I'm stupid. I don't understand people at all.

YELENA. Let's leave it, shall we? And be good friends?

VAGHIN (*laughs*). We'll shake hands on it – yes, why not?

YELENA. Come here. (*Kisses him on the forehead.*) Stay free, Dmitri. For an artist, freedom is as essential as talent or brains. Be truthful, always, and don't take such a dim view of women.

VAGHIN (*touched, but trying not to show it*). You really didn't have to say that, my dear, but, thank you. What you say is true – an artist ought to be alone. Freedom is solitude, after all – *n'est-ce pas?*

YELENA. Yes, it probably is, my friend.

VAGHIN. Pavel's coming. I can hear his ridiculous footsteps. (PROTASOV *enters*.) Well, well – it's my rival!

PROTASOV. Has Melania Nikolaevna gone?

YELENA. She's in the garden with Liza – d'you want me to call her?

PROTASOV. Lena, don't be funny! Listen, take a peep in there – our new maid's trying to eat the soap! I asked her to unwrap a new cake, and she tore off the paper, stuffed it in her pocket, then started licking the soap!

YELENA. Oh, honestly! (*Exits to the house.*)

VAGHIN. Leave her be. We've all got to enjoy ourselves however we can. Like me – I've just been declaring my love to Yelena again.

PROTASOV (*alarmed*). Hm . . . You know, I think you ought to leave, Dmitri, just go away. You'll get over it.

VAGHIN. Oh, I'll go, but I won't get over it, that much I know. But don't concern yourself.

PROTASOV. No no, I'm not worried. Only, well . . . it's a bit awkward.

VAGHIN. What, being happy is awkward? It does you credit, I dare say, but it's pretty stupid.

PROTASOV. Dmitri, don't be angry with me. I mean, this is to do with Lena, it's not my fault. It's just that she loves me, and not you.

VAGHIN (*laughs*). Oh, that's charming!

PROTASOV. No, really, Dmitri, you depressed me terribly yesterday . . . yes, you did! I'm like some sort of planet with no properly defined orbit. I revolve around myself, fly off somewhere or other, and that's it! But you revolve around the sun, you're in harmony with the system . . .

LIZA *enters from the garden, followed by* MELANIA. YELENA *emerges from the house.*

VAGHIN. I've no idea what I'm revolving around, but I'd advise you to start revolving around your wife. Don't let her out of your sight.

PROTASOV. Still, people are wonderful, aren't they.

LIZA (*mournfully*). Hasn't he come yet?

YELENA. No, my dear, he hasn't. Shall I send for him?

LIZA. No, please don't. (*Exits to the house.*)

MELANIA (*quietly, alarmed*). Oh, God, it's as if her mind's wandering. She keeps going on about the steppes, the wilderness . . .

LIZA (*from indoors*). Melania Nikolaevna – where are you?

MELANIA (*hurrying out*). I'm coming, I'm coming . . .

YELENA. Pavel, I'm seriously worried about her. We'd better call the doctor.

PROTASOV. All right, then . . . I'll go.

ANTONOVNA (*enters*). Dmitri Sergeyich, there's a letter here for you.

VAGHIN. Where from?

ANTONOVNA. It's from the flat – it's urgent, they said. (*Exits*)

VAGHIN. What on earth's this? (*He tears open the envelope, begins to read, astonished.*) Good heavens! It's from Chepurnoy – listen to this!

YELENA. Ssshh! Be quiet – Liza . . . What is it?

VAGHIN (*dejectedly*) You know, when he left you yesterday he was laughing and joking, honest to God! And now this . . .

He begins to read, involuntarily slipping into a Ukrainian accent, and imitating CHEPURNOY's *voice.*

'And here's another funny story for you, about the vet who hanged himself. He too wanted to uphold the honour of his profession, like that Englishman. Thank you for drawing that frown-line of mine you found so interesting – it's nice to know that at least something of oneself, even just a wrinkle, is preserved somewhere. Pay more attention to the beauty of your tie – it's important . . . Chepurnoy.'

PROTASOV. Well, that's just silly!

YELENA. Be quiet! What funny story? What's this about? Maybe it's a joke.

VAGHIN. No, hardly. But God damn it, he was laughing!

LIZA (*rushes in, looks round at everybody*). Is he here? Where is he?

YELENA. He's not here.

LIZA. But his voice . . . that was his voice. I heard him speaking just now. Why is everyone silent? Where is he?

VAGHIN. It was me. I was speaking.

LIZA. No. No! It was his voice.

VAGHIN. I was imitating him . . . mimicking his voice.

LIZA. Why?

VAGHIN. Well . . .

PROTASOV. We were just having a chat, you see, and sud-denly . . .

LIZA. What? Suddenly what?

YELENA. Liza, calm down.

VAGHIN. I was recalling his accent, and tried to say a few words in his voice.

LIZA. Really? Is that the truth you're telling me? Then why is everybody silent? Pavel, what's the matter with you? Some-thing's happened, hasn't it? Pavel dearest, you can't tell a lie, can you – what is it?

VAGHIN *slips into the house unobserved.*

PROTASOV. No, Liza, no . . . you see, the fact is . . . um . . . it's true . . . I mean, what Dmitri was saying . . .

YELENA. Liza darling, listen . . .

LIZA. Don't touch me, Yelena! Pavel, you've got to tell me.

PROTASOV. I don't know anything.

LIZA. What does that mean? What don't you know? Yelena, send for him . . . send for Boris right now!

YELENA. Yes, of course – right away. Now, calm down, please.

LIZA. No, no, you're lying about something . . . and where's Dmitri? See, he's talking with his sister . . . and her face . . . look at her face . . .

PROTASOV (*sotto voce, to* YELENA). What are we going to do?

YELENA (*quietly*). Get the doctor, quickly. (PROTASOV *exits.*)

LIZA. I'm going to fall. Yelena, hold me, I'm falling. What were you whispering about?

YELENA. Just about what we can do to calm you. Pavel . . .

LIZA. Where has he run off to? Yelena, for God's sake! Look me in the eye, don't lie to me, Yelena, please!

MELANIA *emerges from the house, followed by* VAGHIN.

Where are you going? Where is he, where's your brother? Where's Boris?

MELANIA. I don't know.

LIZA. No, tell me – tell me straight out – is he dead?

MELANIA. I don't know. I don't know . . . (*Goes towards the gate, and exits.*)

LIZA. No! No! No! Tell me something, anything! My heart's breaking! If he's dead, it's my fault, I've killed him . . . oh, no!

VAGHIN. Liza, the very idea!

MISHA *runs up to the veranda, shouting excitedly, with something akin to joy.*

MISHA. Ladies! Ladies! Mr Vaghin! Have you heard? The vet, Mr Chepurnoy . . .

VAGHIN (*shaking his fist*). Shut up, damn you!

MISHA. He's hanged himself!

LIZA (*breaks free from* YELENA, *then speaks calmly, and distinctly*). Yesterday evening, at about nine o'clock?

MISHA. That's right, yes – on a willow tree, by the little stream. I didn't think you knew.

MISHA *exits.* LIZA, *her eyes wide open and staring. looks at the others, and speaks in a low, strangely meaningful voice.*

LIZA. I knew it . . . do you remember, Yelena? I could feel it . . (*Quietly, horrified.*) No! No! It wasn't me. Tell me I didn't kill him! No! (*Shouts.*) I didn't want that . . . no!

VAGHIN *and* YELENA *pick her up and carry her into the house. She struggles, and keeps repeating the one word 'No!', faster and faster.* ROMAN *enters unhurriedly from around the corner of the veranda, and peers into the house.* LUSHA *comes running out, very frightened.*

LUSHA. Listen – I don't know your name – you're from Ryazan – why are they doing that?

ROMAN. Doing what?

LUSHA. They're dragging the young mistress in, and she's saying no, no!

ROMAN. It's her that's shouting?

LUSHA. Yes, she's screaming, and they're pulling at her. I'm frightened!

ROMAN (*philosophically*). So, what's she shouting about?

LUSHA. I don't know, do I. That's how they are, them folks.

ROMAN. Yes, but there's no need for shouting, is there. That's not right.

MISHA (*comes hurrying round the corner*). Who's doing all the shouting?

ROMAN (*nods towards* LUSHA). It's them indoors.

LUSHA (*waving him away*). What are you looking at me for? It's the gentry.

MISHA (*sternly*). Who was shouting?

LUSHA. The young miss.

MISHA (*giving her a hard look*). What for?

LUSHA. They were dragging her in . . .

MISHA. Who were?

LUSHA. They were, that lot in there.

MISHA (*clapping her on the shoulder*). God, you're as thick as two planks! (*Steps onto the veranda, meets* ANTONOVNA *coming out.*) So, what's happened here, Nanny?

ANTONOVNA. It's Liza, she's had an attack.

MISHA (*to* ROMAN *and* LUSHA). There you are, you see? Numskulls!

ROMAN *slowly walks towards the garden fence, and begins pottering about again.*

So, where did that come from, Nanny?

ANTONOVNA. From God – everything comes from Him!

MISHA (*with a sly smile*). Or maybe from the vet?

Satisfied with himself, MISHA *exits.* ANTONOVNA *watches him go, with a look of reproach, then sighs and shakes her head, pityingly.*

ANTONOVNA. Silly creature. Lusha, what are you doing out here? Go into the house.

LUSHA. Nanny, what sort of attack is it? Is it the falling sickness, or what?

ANTONOVNA. Yes, yes! Now you go inside, d'you hear?

LUSHA. Well, if it's the falling sickness, that's all right, then. I've seen that. Fair gave me a turn, though, when they were dragging the young lady in.

ROMAN *mutters something.* VAGHIN *emerges from the house, frowning. He paces up and down the veranda, looking at ROMAN, then takes out his sketch-pad and a pencil.*

VAGHIN. Hey, old man!

ROMAN. Who, me?

VAGHIN. Yes, you. Stand still a minute.

ROMAN. What for?

VAGHIN (*draws*). I'm trying to draw you.

ROMAN. Well, fancy that. Won't do me any harm, will it?

VAGHIN. There'll be twenty kopecks in it.

ROMAN. That's all right, then.

VAGHIN. Lift your head up a bit.

ROMAN (*does so*). Can do.

VAGHIN. No, no – not so high . . . where d'you think you're going?

ROMAN. Look good to you, do I?

VAGHIN (*sardonically*). Not bad.

A pause. Occasional groans can be heard coming from the house. From a distance, the sounds of a commotion in the streets. MELANIA *enters.*

Well? What is it?

MELANIA (*dully*). I've seen him . . . Terrible . . . His face . . . blue . . . His tongue sticking out . . . as if he was jeering at us, terrible, terrible! How is Liza?

VAGHIN (*gloomily*). You hear her?

MELANIA. How did it all begin? Things were going so well.

VAGHIN. What do you mean, begin?

MELANIA. I don't know. I don't understand anything. Only that it's terrible . . . And you're drawing? How can you do that?

VAGHIN (*not unkindly*). And you're breathing. You can't not breathe, can you. All right, old man, here's your twenty kopecks. (*Flings the money at* ROMAN's *feet.*)

MELANIA. Is Yelena Nikolaevna in there on her own? I'll go in, I might be needed. Oh, God, Boris'll have to be buried and everything. I didn't make any arrangements, I just glanced at him and came straight here. There's some sort of disturbance on the streets, people running about all over the place. I don't understand anything . . . I keep seeing his blue face, swaying back and forth, his tongue sticking out . . . and laughing, laughing! (*begins weeping and goes into the house.*)

ROMAN (*pleased-sounding*). Well, look at that – the lady, she's started crying. What's the matter with her?

VAGHIN. Her brother's dead.

ROMAN. Ah! You don't say? Well, that's all right then, that's good reason. I mean, women cry a lot for nothing, don't they. Give 'em a thump round the head, and they starts howling.

The noise in the streets becomes more distinct. Muffled shouts. Somewhere outside in the yard, a frightened cry from MISHA: 'Roman!'

You'll have to wait. (*Listens.*) It'll be a fire, or maybe somebody getting beaten up. A thief, most like. They've got a hard life too, thieves have. I'd better have a look . . .

YELENA *emerges from the house.* VAGHIN *looks questioningly at her.*

YELENA (*very upset*). I don't think she'll recover.

VAGHIN. Oh, nonsense – this isn't the first time she's been like this, surely?

YELENA. Yes, it is. She's become so cunning now, the way crazy people are. At first she kept asking me to give her poison, then she suddenly went very calm, it was so strange – but she had that cunning glint in her eye, like a wild animal.

VAGHIN. Shall I get you some water?

YELENA. No, thanks. She lay on the bed then, told me I was irritating her. I went into the next room, and suddenly I hear her getting up, so quietly, and walking . . . walking over to Pavel's desk, and there was a revolver in the drawer – look, here it is! I had to fight her for it, she was scratching my arms. Like a wild beast, that's what she was like – a wild animal!

VAGHIN. Good God! And you didn't call me? You didn't cry out?

YELENA. I can't understand it. Honestly, how we didn't shoot each other . . . She's in bed now, we've tied her down, the maid gave me a hand. Nanny just stood there looking on, and crying, she was begging me not to touch Liza, because she's the general's daughter . . . What's that noise? Why are they making so much noise? That sounds very near . . .

VAGHIN. The watchman's gone to find out.

YELENA. And Pavel's not home yet? What's that?

A commotion outside the gates. Shouts are heard: 'Grab him!' 'Aaah!' 'Over the fence!' 'Watch out, lads!' 'Use your stick, will you?' 'Hit him!'

YELENA (*alarmed*). Oh, my God! Let's go!

VAGHIN. No, I'll go.

A DOCTOR *rushes round the corner of the house onto the veranda. He is dishevelled and hatless.*

DOCTOR. For God's sake, hide me! Lock the doors!

YELENA. Doctor, what's the matter?

DOCTOR. There's a riot, they've smashed up the clinic . . . They caught me outside the gates . . . They're going to kill me . . .

VAGHIN rushes towards the gates.

YELENA. Here, take the revolver!

DOCTOR. They'll break in and kill me!

YELENA (*ushers him into the house*). Get inside, quickly! Nanny! Nanny!

A loud crack at the gates – a plank snapped off; the wicket gate is slammed, and there is a sound of glass being smashed. PROTASOV *comes racing in, pursued by about a dozen men. He tries to shoo them away, flapping his hat and handkerchief at them, much to their amusement – some of them burst out laughing.*

PROTASOV. You silly asses! Idiots! Clear off!

FIRST MAN (*from the crowd*). Hey, you hit me in the face with that hanky!

SECOND MAN. Go on, sir, hit him with your hat as well!

THIRD MAN (*angrily*). I'll show you! Don't you call me names!

SECOND MAN. Where's that doctor? Let's find him, lads!

THIRD MAN. This one's a doctor, too – he's got to be!

VAGHIN (*from round the corner somewhere*). Shut the gates! Roman, get rid of these people!

PROTASOV. Don't you dare push me, you fool!

VAGHIN. Pavel! Pavel! Stand firm! I'll give them a beating – clear off, all of you!

Enter YEGOR *and* YAKOV TROSHIN. YEGOR *is slightly tipsy,* TROSHIN *is thoroughly drunk.* YEGOR *rushes up to* PROTASOV *and grabs him by the collar.*

YEGOR. Aha! It's the chemist – caught you nicely, haven't we.

PROTASOV (*pushing him away*). Don't you dare . . .

YEGOR. Lads! Lads! We've got the chief poisoner – he makes the medicines!

PROTASOV. Don't talk rubbish, you cretin! I don't make anything. Help! Somebody help me!

A VOICE. Shout louder! They can't hear you!

YELENA *runs out onto the veranda, and seeing the mob, pulls out the revolver and rushes to her husband's aid.*

YELENA. Yegor, let him go! Get back, Yegor!

PROTASOV. Oh, Lena, Lena!

YEGOR. What, don't you remember? Cholera kills folk, you know. Don't you remember saying . . .

YELENA. Yegor, I'll kill you.

YELENA*'s appearance on the scene prompts several exclamations among the crowd: 'Well, look who's come running out!' 'Hey, lady, you with the pistol!' 'Go on, give her one!' 'You keep your nose out of it!' 'What a woman, eh?'*

YEGOR. Listen, lady – I'm a widower now . . .

YELENA. I'm going to shoot!

YEGOR. And you'll be a widow . . . I'll strangle him!

YELENA *fires. Just before this,* ROMAN *has appeared at the back of the crowd surrounding* YEGOR. *He is carrying a large length of planking. Unhurriedly, he brandishes it in the air and begins beating people over the head with it. He does all this in complete silence, concentrating on his task without a hint of annoyance. At the same moment as* YELENA *shoots at* YEGOR, ROMAN *hits him, and* YEGOR *falls groaning to the ground, dragging* PROTASOV *down with him.* YELENA *advances on the mob, threatening them with her revolver. Following her shot, the mood of the crowd has changed dramatically. Someone calls out in amazement, not very loud: 'She's shot him!' 'Look – Yegor's down!' 'Bitch!' One of the men runs out of the yard, yelling: 'Lads! Lads! They're killing us!' Another runs after him, shouting: 'Don't be such a coward! What're you scared of? It's only a woman . . . ' Almost all of them retreat.*

YELENA (*fearlessly*). Go away! Get out or I'll shoot! Dmitri, where are you? Roman, help my husband! Go away, get out of here! Beasts!

ROMAN *goes up to* TROSHIN, *who is sitting on the ground beside* YEGOR, *mutters something and pulls at* YEGOR, *then hits* TROSHIN *with the plank. The latter moans, and falls over.* VAGHIN *comes running round the corner, very dishevelled and carrying a brick, just in time to see what* ROMAN *is doing.*

VAGHIN. What are you doing, you idiot?

ROMAN. You what?

VAGHIN (*turning towards the crowd*). Yelena! Where's Pavel?

ROMAN *throws away the plank and squats down beside the injured* PROTASOV.

YELENA (*in touch with reality again*). It's him, he's fallen . . . (*Shrieks.*) They've killed him!

VAGHIN. No, it's not possible . . .

MELANIA (*runs out, hearing* YELENA's *cry*). Killed who? Oh, no, it's not true!

YELENA (*aiming the revolver at* YEGOR). It was him. I'll kill him . . .

VAGHIN (*knocks the revolver out of her hand*). What are you doing? Yelena, for God's sake!

MELANIA (*beside* PROTASOV). He's alive! Pavel! Pavel Fyodorovich!

YELENA. Water, give him water!

VAGHIN (*to* MELANIA). Go on, get him some water! Yelena, calm down . . .

MELANIA *runs into the house.*

ROMAN. It's all right. They're all alive. They're moving now, see? Folks get beat up like that all the time, and still live!

VAGHIN *and* YELENA *lift* PROTASOV *to his feet. He is in a dead faint.* ROMAN *gives* TROSHIN *a shove.*

YELENA (*fearfully*). Pavel . . . Pavel . . .

VAGHIN. He's fainted.

ROMAN (*to* TROSHIN). Come on, you, get up! And no funny business, or I'll give you another one.

ANTONOVNA (*running out*). Pasha! Pasha, dearest!

VAGHIN. Nanny, don't shout.

PROTASOV (*semi-conscious*). Lena, is it you? Have they run away? Aah . . .

ANTONOVNA (*to* YELENA). They've killed him . . . You weren't looking after him, were you.

YELENA. Does it hurt? Where does it hurt?

YEGOR *has regained consciousness, lifts up his head and groans.*

ANTONOVNA. Take him in. Carry him into the house.

MELANIA (*bringing the water*). He's come to . . . oh, thank God! Here, drink, drink this.

YELENA. Pavel, tell me – where does it hurt? Did they hit you hard?

PROTASOV. It's all right, I'm not hurting. He was trying to choke me – him, that one. (*Almost fully recovered.*) Lena, are you

all right? I thought somebody had hit you on the head – I
could see a plank coming down . . .

YELENA. No, no, I'm fine – don't worry.

VAGHIN. What about you? Did they hit you?

PROTASOV. No, it wasn't too bad. I don't know why, but they
kept going for my stomach, damn them! What about the
doctor? Is he alive?

MELANIA. Yes, he is. He's on the settee in the drawing-room . . .
he's crying.

YELENA (*fearfully, noticing* ANTONOVNA). Nanny, what about
Liza?

ANTONOVNA. I had to untie her. I couldn't bear to see her
like that.

YELENA. Where is she? Nanny, where is she?

ANTONOVNA (*tearfully*). She's in there. Her dress was all torn. I
had to change her . . .

VAGHIN. What is she doing?

ANTONOVNA. She's looking at a photograph, looking at
him . . .

YELENA. Nanny, go in to her, please!

ANTONOVNA. Pasha ought to be put to his bed. (*Exits, looking
round.*)

PROTASOV (*calls to her*). I'm fine, Nanny! Just had a bit of a
scare, that's all.

MELANIA. Oh, my darling! They've given you a terrible
beating!

PROTASOV. Me? Not at all! I was afraid for her. I thought
somebody fired, and then hit her on the head with a stick, or
a plank, or something . . .

YELENA (*proudly*). Nobody touched me. Come on, let's go inside.

PROTASOV. I managed to defend myself quite successfully. Yes, it's a pity you didn't see any of it. And you know, Lena, it's a pity I took off my galoshes that time – I could've hit them with them!

VAGHIN (*to* YELENA, *with a smile*). You see? Back to his old self.

PROTASOV (*warming to his theme*). Yes, hit them with the galoshes, right in their stupid faces! (*To* YEGOR.) As for you, my dear sir . . .

MELANIA. Now, what's the point of talking to him? Go inside, you need to lie down.

PROTASOV. Please . . .

YELENA. Wait . . . Yegor, did I shoot you?

YEGOR (*dully*). No, you missed. Somebody whacked me on the head.

ROMAN (*proudly*). That was me!

YELENA, *a strained expression on her face, looks at* YEGOR, *then at the others.*

VAGHIN. Oh, yes, you should have seen this sinister machine at work – quite terrifying!

TROSHIN. Kind sirs! I too . . . have a contusion on my head!

ROMAN (*gleefully*). I whacked you as well.

TROSHIN. Gentlemen, I should like you to make a note of that.

YELENA (*peering closely into* YEGOR's *face*). Yegor, do you want some water?

YEGOR. I'd rather have some vodka.

PROTASOV (*to* YEGOR). You . . . you're terribly stupid, my dear sir.

YELENA. Pavel, don't.

PROTASOV. I don't make any medicines whatsoever, damn you!

VAGHIN. Oh, come on, that's enough.

PROTASOV (*tearfully*). No, no, wait! I want to know why he attacked me. What have I ever done to you, Yegor, eh?

YEGOR (*dully*). Nothing. I don't know.

MELANIA. Well, you'll find out at the trial, my friend, you'll hear all about it then!

PROTASOV (*annoyed*). That's enough, really! What trial? You know, I had a very high opinion of you, Yegor. You're a splendid worker, yes! And I paid you well enough, didn't I? So why on earth did you . . .

YEGOR (*stands up, his voice thick with anger*). Don't touch me, master.

YELENA (*firmly*). Pavel, leave him in peace, please.

VAGHIN (*to* YEGOR). You'd better go.

YEGOR (*rudely*). I know. I'm going.

He walks off a little unsteadily. ROMAN *and* TROSHIN *have already moved to the garden fence and are sitting there on the ground, drinking vodka, which* ROMAN *has supplied.* YEGOR *goes up to them in silence, sits down and offers his hand to* ROMAN.

MELANIA. Look at that, an animal!

YELENA. Leave him alone. Come on. Pavel, let's go in.

PROTASOV (*agitated*). No, he's really made me angry. There's something about him, something repellent. People ought to be radiant and bright . . . like the sun . . .

LIZA *comes out onto the veranda. She is wearing a white frock, and her hair is beautifully, but strangely dressed. She walks slowly, with a kind of solemn gait, and a fixed, rather vague, enigmatic smile on her face.*

ANTONOVNA *follows her out.*

LIZA. Goodbye! No, don't say anything, I've made up my mind. I'm leaving! No, please – I don't want to hear any objections. I'm going far away, and for a long time . . . for ever. Do you understand? Listen:

She stops, and then quietly, smiling, begins to read something written on the back of CHEPURNOY's *photograph.*

'Through desert sands my dear love goes,
Through crimson seas, so fiercely burning . . .
And far off in the deep-blue mist, I know,
The wilderness awaits him, filled with yearning . . .
The sun, like someone's evil eye,
Looks on in silence, with its searing gaze . . .
I'll go to join my love, and share his days,
His hard and lonely life, until I die!'

She sings a strange, melancholy tune, very quietly.

'Tall and strong my dear love stands,
And I myself am passing fair;
Like two rare flowers blooming there,
On the vast and lonely sands.'

She falls silent, sighs, then resumes reading.

'And we two, in the burning sun's embrace,
Shall journey through that sandy plain,
And bury deep in some harsh, barren place,
His wasted dreams, and my heart's pain . . . '

LIZA *pauses for thought, and looks at the others. She smiles.*

That's all there is. I wrote it for Boris. Do you know him? Boris? No? (*Walks towards the garden.*) I'm very sorry for you. Really, I'm so sorry . . .

ANTONOVNA *glares at* YELENA, *and follows* LIZA.

YELENA (*quietly, distressed*). Pavel . . . Pavel . . . Do you understand?

PROTASOV (*surprised*). That was beautifully spoken, Liza! Dmitri, you understood, didn't you? That was wonderful!

VAGHIN (*brutally*). She's gone mad, can't you see it?

PROTASOV (*incredulous*). Surely not? Lena?

YELENA (*quietly*). Come on, we'd better go after her . . .

All three go into the garden. YEGOR *is sitting by the hedge, watching them with a look of hatred in his eyes.* TROSHIN *mutters something unintelligible, feeling his head and shoulder with trembling hands.*

ROMAN. That's nothing. I've been beaten worse'n that, and look at me! You want to keep quiet, you do. You're alive, and that's fine . . .

VAGHIN (*Reflectively*) *All alone . . . through desert sands . . . Through crimson seas, so fiercely burning . . .*

Curtain.